"Now that I am almost eighty years old, I take my training seriously when it comes to anything that I do, especially my new passion—pickleball. I am astonished that most older players do not prepare themselves properly before competing in this great sport. This book will not only help you to prepare properly for pickleball but also to prepare for leading a healthier life. I highly recommend everyone read it to reduce the chances of injury and enjoy life to its fullest."

—Rick Barry, NBA Top 50 and Basketball Hall of Fame,
winner of a gold medal at the U.S. Open Pickleball Championships

"The Brungardt brothers, whom I have known for fifteen years, developed an amazing, easy-to-follow plan to help you safely enjoy pickleball."

—Fabrice Gautier, physiotherapist and osteopath for
the French National Basketball Team

"*The Complete Book of Pickleball* is a great road map for balanced athletic development and health for any novice to elite-level athlete."

—Rick Huegli, strength and conditioning coach, NHSSCA Hall of Fame member

"As a physical therapist, I'm seeing more and more pickleball injuries. *The Complete Book of Pickleball* is the perfect resource to help players enhance their overall wellness, reduce injuries, and play pain-free."

—Kate Horrigan, OMPT, New York University

"Pickleball has taken the country by storm! Unfortunately, most players are not physically prepared, and injuries have been rampant—until now! This fun-to-read book will help improve your health and your game. And it will definitely decrease your chance of injuries."

—Bill Foran, Hall of Fame strength and conditioning coach for
the Miami Heat, including three NBA championships

"This book is more than an introduction to pickleball fitness; it is also a plan for wellness and injury prevention for life."

—Sam Sumyk, leading professional tennis coach,
including winners of the Wimbledon, French, and Australian Opens

"I cannot say enough about how much I have learned from the Brungardts in terms of training high-level athletes under unconventional circumstances. This book will help anyone train in the real world with the pressures of a busy, full life and a packed schedule."

—Justin Jackson, expert in NFL and NBA combine training and player development

"Pickleball has taken the world by storm, and these guys know their stuff. Listen to the Brungardt brothers—success has a way of following them. Mike and I worked together to earn two World Championships with the Spurs. I'd go to battle with him anywhere, any day."

—David L. Cook, PhD, author and executive producer of *Seven Days in Utopia*

"This book is an important resource for any pickleball player. For players to stay injury-resistant and play at a high level, pickleball cannot be their only form of exercise."

—Steven Wilde, Wilde Fitness

THE COMPLETE BOOK OF
Pickleball

THE ULTIMATE TRAINING GUIDE FOR PASSIONATE PLAYERS OF ALL LEVELS

Kurt Brungardt, Mike Brungardt, and Brett Brungardt

AVERY

an imprint of Penguin Random House

New York

AVERY

an imprint of Penguin Random House LLC
penguinrandomhouse.com

Most Avery books are available at special quantity discounts for bulk purchase for sales promotions, premiums, fund-raising, and educational needs. Special books or book excerpts also can be created to fit specific needs. For details, write SpecialMarkets@penguinrandomhouse.com.

Library of Congress Cataloging-in-Publication Data

Names: Brungardt, Kurt, author. | Brungardt, Mike, author. | Brungardt, Brett, author.
Title: The complete book of pickleball: the ultimate training guide for passionate players of all levels / Kurt Brungardt, Mike Brungardt, and Brett Brungardt.
Description: New York, NY: Avery, an imprint of Penguin Random House, 2024. | Includes index.
Identifiers: LCCN 2023043624 (print) | LCCN 2023043625 (ebook) | ISBN 9780593715192 (trade paperback) | ISBN 9780593715208 (epub)
Subjects: LCSH: Pickleball (Game)
Classification: LCC GV990.B78 2024 (print) | LCC GV990 (ebook) | DDC 796.34/8—dc23/eng/20231026
LC record available at https://lccn.loc.gov/2023043624
LC ebook record available at https://lccn.loc.gov/2023043625

Printed in the United States of America
1st Printing

Book design by Laura K. Corless

Neither the publisher nor the authors are engaged in rendering professional advice or services to the individual reader. The ideas, procedures, and suggestions contained in this book are not intended as a substitute for consulting with your physician. All matters regarding your health require medical supervision. Neither the authors nor the publisher shall be liable or responsible for any loss or damage allegedly arising from any information or suggestion in this book.

The recipes contained in this book are to be followed exactly as written. The publisher is not responsible for your specific health or allergy needs that may require medical supervision. The publisher is not responsible for any adverse reactions to the recipes contained in this book.

Outdoor recreational activities are by their very nature potentially hazardous. All participants in such activities must assume the responsibility for their own actions and safety. If you have any health problems or medical conditions, consult with your physician before undertaking any outdoor activities. The information contained in this guidebook cannot replace sound judgment and good decision-making, which can help reduce risk exposure, nor does the scope of this book allow for disclosure of all the potential hazards and risks involved in such activities. Learn as much as possible about the outdoor recreational activities in which you participate, prepare for the unexpected, and be cautious. The reward will be a safer and more enjoyable experience.

Accordingly, nothing in this book is intended as an express or implied warranty of the suitability or fitness of any product, service, or design. The reader wishing to use a product, service, or design discussed in this book should first consult a specialist or professional to ensure suitability and fitness for the reader's particular lifestyle and environmental needs.

While the authors have made every effort to provide accurate telephone numbers, internet addresses, and other contact information at the time of publication, neither the publisher nor the authors assume any responsibility for errors, or for changes that occur after publication. Further, the publisher does not have any control over and does not assume any responsibility for author or third-party websites or their content.

Contents

PART 1

Getting Started

Introduction

WHY WE WROTE THIS BOOK

Movement and sports have been part of our lives since we were kids. As career fitness professionals, when we saw more and more people passionately playing pickleball and expressing the desire to move better and avoid injuries, we naturally wondered: What if pickleball players could experience a complete fitness program modeled after pro athlete training camps? This thought inspired us to write *The Complete Book of Pickleball: The Ultimate Training Guide for Passionate Players of All Levels*. The complete training concept sparked us to invite other experts to the pickleball party.

THE TEAM

On the medical side, who better to give health advice than Dr. Josh Dines? The go-to orthopedic surgeon for pro teams like the New York Mets, the Los Angeles Dodgers, the New York Rangers, and the U.S. Davis Cup tennis team, Dines is also (drumroll) the medical director for Major League Pickleball (MLP).

To keep you court-ready, we wrangled longtime San Antonio Spurs athletic trainer

Will Sevening, who has five NBA Championship rings. He offers advice on the day-to-day challenges of staying game-ready.

To achieve the goal of being pain-free, we called on renowned physical therapist Peggy Brill. She will consult on acute pain and apply her concept of "instant relief" to common pickleball aches and pains. She also provides easy exercises you can do right on the court. Back and spine expert Bryon Holmes will explain your spine on pickleball. With over three decades of experience, Holmes knows how to keep your back pain-free and functional.

We brought in a group of innovative young physical therapists from Los Angeles who specialize in the concept of prehab (prevent injuries before they happen) and will change the way you think about PT. Their pickleball specialist Arash Maghsoodi has created a pickleball prehab routine just for you.

To address nutrition, we recruited Jaclyn Sklaver, whose center, Athleats Nutrition, works with pro teams all over the country. Sklaver is the former head of performance nutrition for the Orlando Magic NBA team and was one of the first nutrition experts to create eating strategies for pickleball players. (Her mom, a fellow pickleball pioneer, started playing pickleball over twenty years ago.)

To assess your fitness levels, my middle brother, Brett Brungardt, came aboard to lend his knowledge as a movement and performance specialist. His company, Basic Athletic Measurement (BAM), has tested thousands of athletes of all levels during the past fifteen years. Brett has worked closely with the NBA for over a decade to make their draft combine more reliable. BAM testing provides essential data points for revealing an athlete's strengths and weaknesses. Now he has created a unique set of tests for pickleball.

For your exercise program design, my eldest brother, Mike Brungardt, brings his experience and expertise. Mike served as the strength and conditioning coach for the NBA's San Antonio Spurs for seventeen years. He also trained tennis star Victoria Azarenka (Vika) for two seasons. Mike is a 2011 inductee into the USA Strength and Conditioning Coaches Hall of Fame. He has created a workout program to make any pickler stronger, more athletic, and injury-resistant.

To address the mental side of the game, we enlisted Dr. Patrick Cohn. Dr. Cohn is the founder of Peak Performance Sports. He specializes in the optimal mindset for racquet and paddle sports and coaches elite youth athletes and college and pro tennis players.

For sports vision, Dr. Daniel Laby and Keith Smithson have signed up to advise; both are leaders in the aspects of vision critical for optimal sports performance.

THE PICKLEBALL PORTAL TO THE GOOD LIFE

Finally, we saw an opportunity, through the portal of pickleball, to create a holistic program that would help every pickler live a healthy lifestyle with many payoffs for functional longevity of the body, mind, and spirit.

Body: Create a strong, mobile, agile, athletic, and healthy body.

Mind: Build a positive mindset with a skill set that include positive self-talk, visualization, and tools for resilience—improving well-being on and off the court.

Spirit: Empower the human spirit through sports, wellness, social interaction, and community building.

WHO IS THIS BOOK FOR?

We designed our program for passionate recreational pickleball players with different degrees of fitness experience. Some will have a background in strength training or in high-intensity interval training (HIIT) classes, maybe even yoga or Pilates. Others may be more experienced on the cardio side as runners or bikers. Some users will have a little home gym. Others won't have any equipment. We've accounted for all these variables.

We give you the fundamentals of a complete program, deepen your understanding of and connection to your body, and make you a better pickleball player. The goals of our program are to make you:

- Stronger
- Faster

- More agile (better balance and coordination)
- Mentally tough
- Injury- and pain-free

This book is useful for all ages and varieties of fitness levels—it's for anyone who wants to play pickleball for life. Your passion, combined with our program, will keep you on the court for years to come.

Our companion website has a host of materials to enhance your training experience:

- Videos of all the exercises and drills in the book.
- A training journal to help you organize and track your workouts.
- Additional training techniques and exercises to improve your game.

YOUR PICKLEBALL ATHLETIC JOURNEY

WHAT IT MEANS TO BE PICKLEBALL ATHLETIC (AND WHY YOU SHOULDN'T BE INTIMIDATED)

To be an athlete is to be human. It is to embrace one's sense of play and joy in the body's movement. Like the game of pickleball, this book expands on the idea of what it means to be athletic.

This is the first comprehensive book to view the pickleball player holistically, employing the same methods and techniques used by pro athletes. We emphasize improving performance and staying injury-free. We guide the player step by step from simple to more challenging workouts and training techniques. Even more, our system will enhance both your longevity and the quality of your life.

In our culture, the terms *athlete* and *athletic* can be intimidating and can generate anxiety. They can throw you back to being picked last at recess or cut from your high school team. They can even evoke feelings of low self-esteem or body image issues. For some, however, these words might be inspiring and positive, even aspirational.

Positive feelings around playing sports and engaging in a regular fitness and wellness program can transform your life. Our training system, along with your pickleball court time, are the two components of a lifelong athletic journey. Our team will treat you like a pro, building your confidence and guiding you through this process.

A TOUR OF YOUR TRAINING JOURNEY AND THE PB-150 PROGRAM

This book is designed to be a portable version of a bricks-and-mortar elite pickleball sports performance training center. As your coaches, we will train you like a multimillion-dollar pro athlete with the same long-term fitness goals as legendary players like Tom Brady and LeBron James (both of whom own pro pickleball teams). You will enjoy the same high-level expertise, along with appropriate commonsense modifications.

TESTING: A SNAPSHOT OF YOUR PICKLEBALL FITNESS

Typically, for an athlete, the journey begins with testing to obtain benchmarks. We've developed innovative pickleball combine tests designed to mirror those used at the NBA and NFL draft combines. For those not familiar with the term, a sports combine is a series of athletic tests that measure speed, agility, reaction time, and power. Sound intimidating? The process is actually fun. The tests reveal your strengths and weaknesses, and these data points will help focus your training program and keep you motivated along the way.

THE SEVEN PB-150 COMPONENTS

We call it PB-150 (for pickleball 150 minutes a week). It's more than just a single isolated workout—it's synergistic; the whole is greater than the sum of its parts, creating a holistic program that positively impacts your whole person—mind, body, and spirit.

The number 150 represents the number of minutes you must devote each week to complete all program components (altogether, this is fewer than three hours a week). This duration is based on what exercise scientists consider the minimum amount to gain the health and wellness benefits of exercise. We know you are also playing pickleball, so we designed our program around managing the load, using your time efficiently, and including elements important for injury prevention and recovery.

Let's start by looking at PB-150's seven components.

PREHAB

To decrease your chances of injury, your program includes a prehab routine. The practice of prehabilitation has expanded from something you do before surgery to something you proactively employ to *avoid* injuries and the need for medical intervention. Your pickleball prehab routine is a unique sequence of exercises that focus on the key joints and areas susceptible to pickleball-specific damage.

DYNAMIC WARM-UP

The dynamic warm-up is a sequence of movements that prepares the body for the court. It also challenges and improves balance, coordination, joint mobility, and stability. Unlike static stretching or riding on a stationary bike for five minutes, our dynamic warm-up involves continuous, controlled movements that relate to pickleball.

STRENGTH TRAINING

The strength training component will add power to the body's fundamental movement patterns: push, pull, squat, lunge, hinge, and overhead press. This program is designed to be safe and effective for all fitness levels.

PICKLEBALL DRILLS

We include drills designed to improve movement skills for pickleball. These drills will boost agility, speed, coordination, balance, reaction time, and overall athleticism. The drills will enhance your ability to move in multiple directions and in all three planes of motion.

CORE TRAINING

Your core is crucial to maintaining proper posture, supporting the spine, and enabling efficient movement and balance. The core muscles work together to stabilize the body during athletic movements, functioning as the hub for transferring speed and power from the ground up and in all directions, helping improve all phases of your game.

FOAM ROLLING

Foam rolling is our preferred method of soft tissue work. We will teach you a quick and effective technique to create and maintain healthy connective tissue surrounding every part of your body, aka, fascia.

COOLDOWN

The last component is recovery. Our sequence will incorporate stretches to improve your flexibility and integrate breathing techniques to start the recuperation process.

PICKLEBALL WELLNESS

In this part of the book we'll look at pickleball from a sports and wellness perspective. We have chapters on nutrition, sports psychology, and sports medicine that include important methods for eating better, reducing stress, developing a winning mindset, improving sports vision, and staying game-ready and pain-free.

HOW TO USE THIS BOOK

We've done two things to make this book user-friendly. We've created an easy-to-follow program and an open and flexible system so that you can sync it with your changing weekly schedule.

A useful way to approach the book is to think of it as a combination of doing and reading. Each will inform and deepen the other.

ATHLETICISM AND THE BEAUTY OF THE GAME

As you launch into your journey, let's revisit what it means to be an athlete—experiencing the beauty of the game and the beauty of the human body at rest and in motion.

To be an athlete means to move well and strive for a functionally strong body, which we (the authors) say is beautiful. These ideas come together in Michelangelo, the great artist of the human body. He exemplifies beauty in two sculptures, David and Moses. David is a model for beauty, the perfect man (yet he is not perfectly symmetrical, giving all of us a reprieve), but our focus is the lesser-known sculpture of Moses.

In Moses, Michelangelo created a figure ready for action. A closer look is inspiring, especially as analyzed by Dr. Beth Harris and Dr. Steven Zucker. These two are groundbreaking and insightful art historians, and it is clear from their analysis that they would also make great personal trainers and pickleball coaches. Their work in art history has democratized art education, similar to the way pickleball has democratized sports. They describe Michelangelo's Moses as follows:

> *The entire figure is charged with thought and energy . . . Moses is not simply sitting down; his left leg is pulled back to the side of his chair as though he is about to rise. And because this leg is pulled back, his hips also face left. Michelangelo [creates] an interesting, energetic figure—where the forces of life are pulsing throughout the body.*

In short, Moses is in a ready position, his body loaded and prepared to spring into action. You can also see his inner life. He's like an athlete getting ready to fly off the bench and into the game. Or more pertinently, a pickleball player who is ready to enter the court.

The point here is that being a pickleball athlete is expansive. Like the game itself, pickleball athleticism encompasses all ages, fitness levels, and body types. It integrates a strong, functional body (the goal of this book) and the playful and expressive beauty of the game.

Let the journey begin . . .

2.

TRAINING PRIMER

KNOW THYSELF

Playing pickleball and engaging in an exercise program are both portals to a greater understanding of yourself and your body. From playing pickleball, you've already developed a deeper connection with your body and recognize its strengths and limitations. You've experienced the high of playing a competitive game, making impressive volley returns, hitting a powerful ground stroke for a winning game, as well as the postgame exhilaration, similar to a runner's high. In pickleball, you have also enjoyed the camaraderie of the court. By contrast, you may also have experienced the soreness that comes with pushing your limits on the court. Don't worry, we'll show you how to recover properly and be ready for whatever tomorrow has to bring.

You can become your own trainer for life, but this requires a certain base of knowledge. What follows are key concepts and methods for training.

Intellectually, we know why we should exercise. Exercise is the one evidence-based activity that provides undeniable benefits for your mood and brain health and protection against almost all the major illnesses. Yet according to a 2018 survey by the U.S. government, 50 percent of adults and 73 percent of high school students don't meet minimal levels of physical activity. What's more, 70 percent of adults report they never exercise in their leisure time.

Dr. Daniel E. Lieberman, a Harvard anthropologist, has spent his career studying exercise through the lens of anthropology. Lieberman defines exercise as "voluntary physical activity that is planned, structured, repetitive, and undertaken to sustain or improve health and fitness." Back in the day, labor for hunter-gatherers and early farmers was physical. They moved in a variety of ways for work and walked long distances to hunt and gather food. Unlike us, they didn't sit behind desks most of the day and get from place to place in cars. Their energy was conserved for work and reproduction, not a HIIT class or hot yoga. Lieberman explains that we as a species did not evolve to exercise.

WHY EXERCISE?
THE BALANCED BODY

It's probably a safe bet that many of you purchased this book because you struggle to stay consistently engaged in an exercise program. It's a case of knowing better and doing worse. But now your passion for pickleball can be your portal into regular exercise. And if you are already a consistent exerciser, pickleball is a way to level up your fitness practices. And, yes, there are excellent reasons why you should supplement pickleball with an exercise regimen.

A proper exercise program will address muscular balance throughout your body, which a sports activity will not do. Almost any sport you play will use certain muscle groups extensively while other muscle groups serve only a supporting role. As we have stressed, a proper exercise program will help offset these imbalances and keep you injury-free. Muscular balance allows the body to stay healthy and avoid many unnecessary injuries. It will also help you play at a higher level, increasing your enjoyment of pickleball.

THE WARM-UP

Warming up before exercise is essential. It will:

- Increase the blood flow to your muscles, allowing them to work more efficiently.
- Increase the temperature of your muscles, allowing them to contract more forcefully and faster. In other words, your workouts will be more intense.
- Prepare your body and joints to move in all directions.
- Reduce your chance of injury.

In our program, we start each workout with either a prehab or dynamic warm-up component.

TRAINING TERMS, TECHNIQUES, AND CONCEPTS

REPS: Repetition is the completion of one cycle of an exercise. If you have completed 10 squats, then you have completed 10 repetitions. Repetitions are also referred to as reps.

SETS: A set is a consecutive series of repetitions. If you perform 10 repetitions of a squat, then rest, and then perform 10 more repetitions of the squat, you have completed 2 sets of 10 repetitions (2 × 10).

PHASES: A phase in strength training is a period of time during which specific exercises, sets, and reps are prescribed. Each phase has a goal. The phases we have designed for you are generally four weeks long, with some including two-week prep phases.

TYPE OF TRAINING: How you train should match your goals. For pickleball, your goals include strength, power, speed, and agility. PB-150 matches these goals. This is radically different from the type of training you would do to run a marathon.

UNDERSTANDING THE BODY ON EXERCISE: ADAPTATION

GENERAL ADAPTATION SYNDROME

Physiologically, an exercise program aims to expose the muscles to a stress or an increased workload to stimulate positive adaptations: you get stronger and faster and have more stamina.

The general adaptation syndrome (GAS), which was developed by Dr. Hans Selye, has become a staple for understanding physical development. GAS has three distinct stages.

Alarm Stage: This is the initial response to a stress or stimulus. For us, this stress is engaging in workouts and playing pickleball. The body's first response to this can be fatigue and soreness. We want to minimize this—but a little soreness is normal.

Resistance Stage: This is the body's positive adaptive response to training. In pickleball, the body gets better conditioned: stronger, faster, more agile, and more skilled on the court, as a response to your training. This is the goal of physical conditioning.

Exhaustion Stage: This is the body's negative response to a workload that's too intense. Here the body no longer has the capacity to adapt positively during training or on the court. The tank is empty. You are overtraining, not giving your body enough rest and recovery. Overtraining can lead to:

- Decreased performance level
- Chronic fatigue
- Loss of appetite
- Loss of body weight or lean body mass
- Increased potential for illness
- Increased potential for injury
- Decreased motivation and loss of self-esteem

During this stage, desired training adaptations will not occur. Outside stresses also need to be considered. Sleep, social life, nutrition, work—all impact your performance.

The goal is to remain in the resistance stage, where your body positively adapts to stress by making gains.

OVERLOAD AND PROGRESSION: For your body to develop and your muscles to get stronger, you have to overload them. Overloading a muscle involves applying stress to a muscle greater than what it is used to. Progression is a planned method of overloading. Standard methods for creating progressive overload include adding weight, reps, or sets to a program to create positive adaptations. This means you have to be willing to push yourself in a safe way.

ACTIVE REST: As a pickleball player, you can think of active rest as your off-season. It can be between two and four weeks. You stay active but give your body a break from the repetitive activity of playing pickleball and from your organized training program. In PB-150 this is scheduled in as your transition phase. Active rest is designed to prevent overtraining, so you should get out of the weight room and even off the pickleball court and do different activities. The following are guidelines for active rest:

After each season (three to four months of playing), take one to two weeks of active rest.

After twelve to fifteen consecutive weeks of strength training, take one week of active rest.

Active rest does not mean sitting on the couch and watching TV: take a yoga or Pilates class, ride a bike, hike, play miniature golf.

You can continue to foam roll and do prehab and a dynamic warm-up.

FREQUENCY OF TRAINING

The frequency of training depends on many variables, including recovery time, your physiology, your level of experience, and your athletic goals. Recovery time is an important factor in determining how often you work out. You gain strength and your muscles grow during recovery periods. If you don't allow your body to recover between workouts, then your strength gains will decrease. You will also be at risk for overtraining.

As a general guideline, we advocate for strength training two days a week, with 48 to 72 hours between sessions (for example, Monday and Thursday for strength). Drills and conditioning should be done two days a week, also with 48 to 72 hours between sessions (for example, Tuesday and Friday for drills and conditioning). It's okay to just have 24 hours' rest between prehab, dynamic warm-up, cooldown, and foam rolling sessions. In fact, you can do these workouts on consecutive days. Keep these basic recovery principles in mind as you plan your week.

What time of day you exercise is up to you. For some, early morning is best, while others prefer the evening, and depending on their schedule, some like late morning or early afternoon. Any of these are fine as long as they allow you to be consistent.

TRAINING TECHNIQUE

Technique is critical to the success of your program. Proper technique will give the best and safest results in the least amount of time. We'll provide the cues and tips you need to achieve proper technique.

BREATHING

Breathing when exercising or doing any activity is essential to stay energized and efficient in your movements. In yoga class, the instructor constantly reminds you to breathe into each posture. During exercise, the rule of thumb is to exhale during the working portion of the exercise, or when you are moving against the most resistance or against gravity. Inhale when you're moving against the least resistance to refuel by bringing in fresh oxygen. For example, on a push-up you exhale as you push your body away from the floor and inhale as you lower your body back down to the floor.

FULL RANGE OF MOTION

Be sure to perform each exercise through a full range of motion. Though it's tempting to make short, quick movements, we want to train and strengthen the muscle group through its full range. This ensures your strength training supports your athletic performance. All athletic skills are either dynamic or isometric in nature. Because your on-court movements are dynamic, you need to train your muscles dynamically, and through a full range of motion. Your joints will become more flexible and stronger at both ends of a movement—preparing your body for the rigors of pickleball. This also reduces chances of injury.

SPEED OF MOVEMENT: THREE SPEEDS

STANDARD SPEED

As a general rule, no matter how fast or slow your exercise movement is, you need to maintain proper technique throughout the full range of motion. Slower speeds help keep tension in the muscles. Control the negative phase of the lift, where gravity is trying to take the weight down. This would be done to a 3-count. The positive phase, where the exercise requires overcoming gravity, would be done to a 2-count.

SLOW

This means you perform both phases slowly. A 5-second negative phase and a 5-second positive phase are good guidelines.

FAST

This means you perform the positive phase as explosively as possible, maintaining good technique. You would still control the negative phase to a 2- to 3-count, followed by a fast and powerful positive phase to a 1-count or even less.

As you get more advanced, and depending on the reason for doing the exercise, you may choose to vary the speed:

- to create variety.
- to train for sports-specific movements.
- to train for explosiveness and speed.
- to train a movement utilizing a different energy system.

PICKLEBALL ENERGY SYSTEMS

Every physical activity you do requires energy. The energy expenditure varies depending on the type and intensity of the activity. As a sport, pickleball requires speed, agility, and quick reflexes. It demands short bursts of power for volleying, smashing, and getting to the net.

In exercise physiology language, energy systems are the metabolic pathways responsible for generating the energy you need for your activity. There are three energy systems, and in pickleball you tap into all three. That's why PB-150 incorporates all three energy systems into your workout. We'll help you understand how they work and how to apply them to the game.

THE THREE SYSTEMS

Explosive System

In exercise physiology, the explosive system is known as the phosphagen or ATP system. It is the primary energy source for intense, explosive movements like sprinting and jumping. Its drawback is that the ATP energy lasts only up to ten seconds. Many key pickleball moves depend on this system: quick volleys at the net, overhead smashes, powerful ground strokes, and springs to the ball to make a shot.

Sustained Power System

In exercise physiology, the anaerobic or glycolytic system provides sustained power. It supplies energy for vigorous activities lasting up to two minutes, such as high-intensity interval training (HIIT). The sustained power system kicks in after the explosive system runs out of juice, providing needed energy. Your body draws from this energy system for long rallies and back-to-back points with sustained rallies.

Endurance System

In exercise physiology, this is known as the aerobic system. It is the main source of energy for low-intensity, long-duration activities such as distance running, cycling, and swimming— or a long afternoon of pickleball. This system also helps the other two systems function efficiently.

PB-150 program elements allow you to focus on training the energy system that matches the demands of the game, which is key to your success on the court.

TOOLS FOR TWEAKING: EASING BACK, LEVELING UP

This section will give you basic tools to apply when tweaking your routine to match your current lifestyle. They will in effect empower you to become your own performance coach and help guide your decision-making. You will evaluate whether to ease back or level up based on the following variables.

INTENSITY = HOW HARD

A simple way to judge intensity is to ask yourself how quickly you reach failure in an exercise. The faster you reach failure, the greater the intensity.

Let's look at an example with the squat. On your first set, you do 20 reps using 50 pounds as a warm-up. On your second set, you do 5 reps using 100 pounds. The second set is more intense; you reach failure much faster. There are three main ways to increase intensity:

Increase the difficulty level of the exercise.

Increase the amount of resistance used in the exercise.

Increase or decrease the rest time between exercises.

VOLUME = HOW MUCH

The volume combines the total number of repetitions and sets in your workout. Don't increase volume and intensity at the same time. When you increase intensity, your volume needs to decrease, and vice versa. For example, you shouldn't add a more difficult exercise at the same time as you increase the number of sets in your routine. Add only one challenging element at a time.

REST AND RECOVERY =
AMOUNT OF REST BETWEEN WORKOUTS

You probably are starting to see how all these variables are connected, how one affects another. Rest is related to frequency, volume, and intensity. The greater the volume, intensity, and frequency, the more you'll have to be diligent about rest time. You get stronger on your days off. Make sure to use all your recovery tools: sleep, nutrition, supplements, and foam rolling.

VARIETY =
MAKING A CHANGE TO CREATE POSITIVE ADAPTATION

Intelligent variety is one of the most neglected training principles. Training needs to be varied to create positive adaptations and prevent training plateaus. Intelligent variety consistently challenges the body. This needs to be done thoughtfully, not creating chaos or confusion. There are several ways to create variety:

Increase the resistance.
Increase the number of sets.
Increase the number of exercises.
Change the exercise.

APPLYING THE VARIABLES

As a general rule, add one variable at a time, and make choices to fit your goals and training needs. For example, don't increase your weight on an exercise and decrease your rest time simultaneously. This would be adding two elements of intensity at once. Just one will challenge your body to adapt and grow stronger at the optimal pace. If you add both, you overstress your body and give away all your tricks at once. You want slow, steady progress, not burnout and injury.

The PB-150 does all this work for you. Understanding these concepts will give you a deeper comprehension of the process, which can help you keep your eye on the prize. Knowledge is power!

QUESTIONS FOR SELF-ASSESSMENT

Innovative physical therapist Gary Gray famously said, "The exercise is the assessment, and the assessment is the exercise." It would be nice to have Gray at your side, observing your workout, but his idea can empower you, even as a beginner. Doing the exercises in your workout gives you useful feedback about your body's strengths and weaknesses. To self-assess, ask yourself these questions:

1. Can I do the exercise pain-free?

    Before you answer, let's distinguish between good pain and bad pain.

    Good pain is the feeling of your muscles and movements being challenged in a positive way. In short, the move is demanding; you feel your muscles and joints working, and you are fatigued at the end of your set.

    Bad pain is when you feel a sharp pain, a shooting pain, tingling or numbness, a spasm, a strain, or a pop—anywhere in your body. These are red flags and a signal that you should immediately stop the exercise.

2. Can I get through a full range of motion for the move?

    The full range means you can do the exercise as described. For example, when you squat, your hips are parallel to the ground.

3. Can I do the exercise correctly without compensation?

For example, on the squat, you move through a full range of motion without your heels coming off the ground. For a shoulder press, you can fully extend your arms above your head while maintaining correct alignment.

4. Can I do the exercise in a balanced and fluid motion?

   You should feel balanced, coordinated, and confident.

5. Am I progressing with the exercise?

   Progress simply means you've been able to add more weight and/or reps.

PATIENCE AND PERSEVERANCE

You want to answer yes to all these questions. If you're having a mobility issue with a particular area (ankles, hips, shoulders), be sure to include a set of exercises that addresses that area in your prehab routine. As a general note, any exercise you struggle with in any of the components (dynamic warm-up, prehab, strength, conditioning drills, foam rolling, and cooldowns) is an exercise exposing a weakness. Give a little extra attention to this area and be patient with these moves. Focus on one area of the body at a time. PB-150 has been designed to bring, over time, every area of your body back to full function.

3.

COMBINE TESTING:
DISCOVERING YOUR FITNESS LEVEL

You may be familiar with combine events for the NBA and NFL drafts. At this event, potential draft picks sprint, jump, and dash agilely around cones. The goal is to evaluate the strengths and weaknesses of the athlete's potential as a draft choice. In addition, these numbers can be utilized as benchmarks for training. With the goal of training you like a pro athlete, we've created a pickleball-specific combine to help you discover your strengths and find out where you may need improvement.

Don't be intimidated by the tests. They can be fun and, at the same time, teach movement literacy. Don't be too hard on yourself if your times aren't as fast as you'd like. Testing is a snapshot, just one tool in determining success. Its greatest use is in laying out a path to success in physical development. Many successful athletes did not have great combine results but were highly skilled both mentally and physically in the specifics of their sport.

TESTING IS YOUR BODY'S GPS FOR PERFORMANCE

We often relate testing to the global positioning system (GPS) on your smartphone. GPS tells you where you are. And in order to reach your performance goals, you need to know where you're starting from. Pickleball combine tests will provide these metrics. PB-150 will then put you on a route to improving them.

Benefits of Testing

Baseline measurements for benchmarking: Testing will give you a snapshot of your present level.

Back-to-play guidelines: If you suffer an injury or a setback, testing numbers can help you determine when to get back on the court.

Indication of overtraining/exhaustion: If your numbers are suffering a downward trend, that data can also be a sign that you're overdoing it.

Determination of your weak link: What is your lowest score? This tells you what area needs the most work. Improving this weak link can bring up your scores in other areas.

WHAT WE TEST

The Pickleball combine is based on the Basic Athletic Measurement (BAM Testing) platform, utilizing five tests that measure athletic performance:

- Speed
- Agility
- Reaction
- Power
- Local muscular endurance

WHEN TO TEST

As a general rule, you should test at the beginning and end of a training cycle. For example, test before you begin PB-150; then test again after you have completed the three-month cycle, to evaluate results. The process is simple: test, train, and retest. This allows you to see if your training is helping you reach your goals.

HOW TO SET UP YOUR PICKLEBALL COMBINE

For reliable testing, you must repeat the tests the same way each time. Following the same steps for each test will help guarantee reliable results. Just as the NBA utilizes a basketball court and the NFL a football field, we have designed these tests to be done on a pickleball court. If a pickleball court is unavailable, the dimensions of the court in each test are available on the illustrations. For best results, please try to find a surface similar to that of a pickleball court—that is to say, not dirt or grass.

YOUR PICKLEBALL PARTNER

To test, team up with a partner who can record your times.

For consistency, we'll position where your partner should stand with the timer.

For each test, you will rotate. You test. They time. Then you switch places.

This is true for all tests except the broad jump. For this test, you do both trials consecutively.

Once you have both completed a test, move on to the next test in the order prescribed.

You always use your best time.

The diagram for each test will help guide you through the steps with arrows. You can also use our YouTube link to see a short video for each.

THE TESTS

🎾 FOUR-WAY AGILITY: SETUP AND GUIDELINES

What Gets Measured
- Multidirectional speed and agility.

Equipment Needed
- 4 cones, each 12 inches tall.
- Stopwatch, smartphone, or laser timing gate.
- Helper: To keep time at the finish line.

Trials
- 2 attempts with a 1-minute rest between trials.

Setup
- On the pickleball court, place one cone inside each of the four corners of the combined left and right service areas (see diagram).

PERFORMING THE TEST

Starting Position
- Pickler starts in the upper left-hand corner of the left service area (intersection of sideline and non-volley zone/kitchen line).
- Pickler must begin the drill with hips and shoulders perpendicular to the net and stay facing this direction throughout the test.

The Movement
- Run forward, lateral slide, backward, and lateral slide (in a square pattern around the court).
- Sprint along the net adjacent service area line toward the right service area, to the next adjacent right service area and sideline intersection (cone 1).

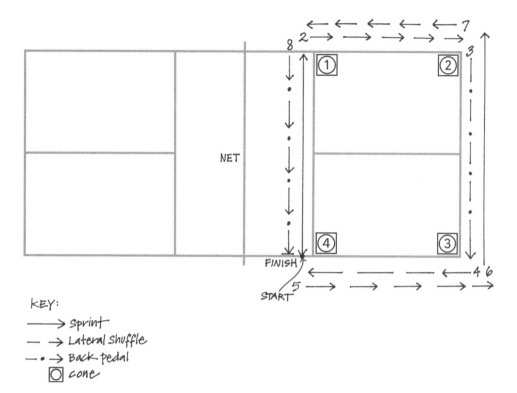

KEY:

⟶ Sprint

– ⟶ Lateral Shuffle

–•⟶ Back pedal

☐ Cone

- Transition around the cone and perform a right lateral slide (facing the same direction, the pickler moves in a lateral direction—left to right without crossing legs/feet) along the sideline to the baseline intersection of the right service area (cone 2).
- Transition around the cone into a backpedal along the baseline adjacent service area line toward the left service area lane and sideline intersection (cone 3).
- Transition around the cone into a left lateral slide (facing the same direction, the pickler moves in a lateral fashion—right to left without crossing your legs/feet) along the sideline to the net adjacent intersection of the left service area (starting corner, cone 4), and touch parallel with the cone at the starting position. This is the halfway point.
- The pickler then changes direction into a right lateral slide along the left service area sideline to cone 3.
- Transition around the cone into a forward sprint along the baseline to the intersection of the right service area and sideline (cone 2).

- Transition around the cone into a left lateral slide along the sideline toward the net adjacent right service area and sideline intersection (cone 1).
- Transition around the cone into a backpedal along the net adjacent service area line toward the left service area lane and sideline intersection (start/finish corner, cone 4).

The Finish

- Finish by crossing the start/finish line.

Disqualifications

- Crossing of the feet during a lateral slide.
- Cutting a corner/touching a cone.
- Not getting to the return point with the foot at the midway point of the drill.
- Falling down (falling through the finish line is acceptable, provided it is without touching a cone).

🏓 REACTION SHUTTLE: SETUP AND GUIDELINES

What Gets Measured

- Reaction, agility, and ability to change directions.

Equipment Needed

- 4 cones, each 12 inches tall, or 4 pickleballs.
- Stopwatch, smartphone, or laser timing gates.
- Helper: To keep time.

Trials

- 2 attempts with a 30-second rest between trials.

Setup

- On the court, timer stands at net; pickler stands at start/finish.

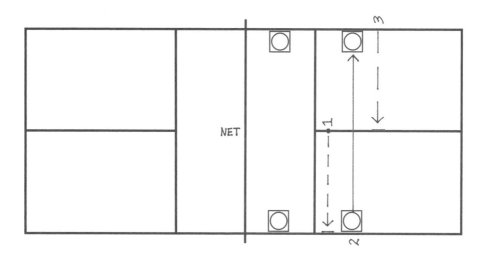

KEY:
——→ Sprint
— — → Lateral Shuffle
— • → Back pedal
◻ cone

PERFORMING THE TEST

Starting Position

- Pickler stands at the kitchen line, straddling the center line. This intersection of the center and kitchen lines (1) marks the start and finish.
- This is a reaction test, and the timer has another responsibility. The timer faces and stands directly in front of the pickler at the net (lightly touching the net) with both arms hanging naturally to their sides. The stopwatch will always remain in the same hand for all the trials of the test.

The Movement

- As directed by the timer, move left or right to the sideline and touch with the appropriate foot. If you are directed to move to your right, you must touch that sideline with your right foot. If you are directed to move to your left, you must touch that sideline with your left foot. (Do not turn your back to the net.) Then run across the starting line to the opposite sideline, switching directions again, and run back through the starting position to complete the test.

- Once the pickler is in the correct starting position, the timer will hold the pickler in the starting position for 2 to 5 seconds. This time will vary or be random between all trials.
- At the chosen count, the starter will raise either the right arm or the left arm directly out to the side, simultaneously starting the stopwatch and moving the appropriate arm to point the direction the pickler will go.
- The pickler reacts and must touch the outside of the service area that the timekeeper pointed to, left or right, with the correct foot (see diagram). The pickler can use any strategy to accomplish this—turn and sprint, side shuffle, etc.
- The pickler then transitions into a sprint in the opposite direction, across the start/finish line, to touch the opposite lane line with the correct foot (see diagram).
- The pickler then transitions into a sprint in the opposite direction, to cross the start/finish line (see diagram).
- The pickler completes a total of 3 trials. Always have the pickler's first move tested in both directions. The fastest time is recorded, with one false start allowed.

The Finish

- Finish by crossing the start/finish line.

Disqualifications

- Premature start.
- Wrong direction at the start.
- Turning your back to the net.
- Missing a line.
- Falling down.

🏓 STANDING BROAD JUMP: SETUP AND GUIDELINES

What Gets Measured

- Power—how many feet you can jump.

Equipment Needed

- 16-foot measuring tape.
- Yardstick or ruler.
- Helper: To mark landing.

Trials

- 2 consecutive attempts.

Setup

- On the court, place the tape measure parallel to the baseline/service area sideline intersection, with the outside of the baseline providing the start line (zero) (see diagram).

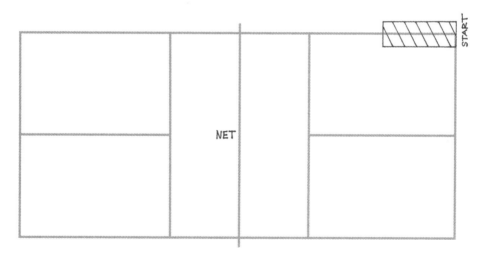

PERFORMING THE TEST

Starting Position

- The pickler must begin with both feet/toes totally behind the start line (baseline/service area intersection) for a valid jump.

The Movement

- The pickler may swing arms and bend knees prior to jumping.
- Upon landing, the pickler must maintain control, landing balanced with both feet planted.
- Upon landing, the pickler may also fall forward but must keep feet stationary or planted. The pickler may not fall backward.

The Finish

- Jumps are measured from the heel of the foot nearest to the initial jump line by placing the yardstick behind the heel perpendicular to the tape measure.
- Jumps are measured to the nearest ½ inch.
- Results are recorded in total inches jumped.

Disqualifications

- The pickler falls backward after landing the jump.
- The pickler steps past the line before the jump.
- The pickler steps into the jump.
- After the first disqualification, the pickler is allowed to retry the jump.

POWER CORE: SETUP AND GUIDELINES

What Gets Measured

- Upper body strength/endurance—core stability.

Equipment Needed

- Stopwatch or smartphone; 1 pickleball.

Helper

- Stands directly in front of the planked athlete.

Trial

- 1 attempt.

Variations

- 15 reps for male picklers, 12 reps for female picklers.

Setup

- On the court, helper stands ready to keep time.

PERFORMING THE TEST

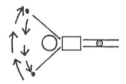

Starting Position

- The pickler assumes the plank push-up position; feet are on the baseline. Each hand and foot straddles the center line, with hands and feet equidistant from the center line. Arms are fully extended, hands are directly beneath shoulders, and a pickleball is held between the knees (see diagram). If you feel uncomfortable or if the test is too difficult from this position, use the modified position.
- Modified Position: In the same position on the court, the pickler assumes the planked push-up position; but instead of being on the toes, the muscles just above the knees support the weight of the body, creating a straight line through the knees, hips, shoulders, and ears (the position of the head can move during the test). A pickleball is placed between the knees.

The Movement

- While maintaining a plank position and keeping the ball in place, the pickler will lift one hand to touch the other, repeating the required number of reps.
  - The pickler begins by moving the right hand laterally across the center line and touching the left hand. The movement of the right hand starts the clock.
  - Pickler proceeds by moving the right hand back to the approximate starting position and moves the left hand laterally to touch the top of the right hand— this counts as one rep.
  - Pickler repeats this pattern until they have completed the required number of repetitions: 15 for men and 12 for women (if the pickler has to stop and rest, that is okay).

The Finish

- Once the left hand touches the top of the right hand on the final correctly performed repetition, the clock is stopped.

Disqualifications

- Excessive piking of hips.
- Any knee(s) touching the ground (except in the modified position).
- Dropping the pickleball.
- Repetitions are not counted when the pickler does not touch the opposite hand with the lateral movement, or when the returning hand does not cross the center line.

🏓 PICKLEBALL SPRINT: SETUP AND GUIDELINES

What Gets Measured

- Linear speed and power.

Equipment Needed

- 4 Cones, 12 inches tall, or 4 pickleballs.
- Stopwatch or timing gates.

Helper

- Stands facing the finish line, with timing device.

Trials

- 2 attempts with a 30-second rest between trials.

Setup

- Pickler will run parallel to the sideline of the court, so place 2 pickleballs or cones to mark the baseline and the kitchen line on the other side of the net (see diagram).

PERFORMING THE TEST

Startinwition

- The pickler is instructed to take a two-point staggered stance with the front foot behind the edge of the baseline or the pickleballs.

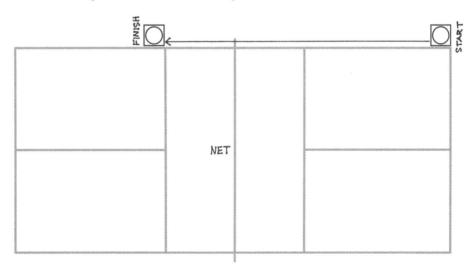

KEY:

———→ Sprint

— —→ Lateral shuffle

—·—→ Back pedal

▢ cone

- The pickler must begin with hips and shoulders square to the finish line.

The Movement
- The pickler choses when to begin, with the timekeeper (who is stationed even with the finish line) starting the stopwatch on the pickler's first movement.
- The pickler sprints to the finish line to complete the test.

The Finish
- The pickler crosses the finish line (the kitchen line on the other side of the net).

Disqualifications
- The pickler makes a false/premature start.
- The pickler rocks back and forth before starting.
- The pickler stumbles.
- The pickler makes an extraneous movement.
- The pickler falls.

WHAT THE NUMBERS MEAN

Below are times and corresponding levels for your results. Find your time, then move to the right to get your level.

Four-Way Agility

MEN		WOMEN	
0.00–10.68 seconds:	Level 7	0.00–11.48 seconds:	Level 7
10.60–11.34 seconds:	Level 6	11.49–12.14 seconds:	Level 6
11.35–13.02 seconds:	Level 5	12.15–13.72 seconds:	Level 5
13.03–14.34 seconds:	Level 4	13.73–15.03 seconds:	Level 4
14.35–16.83 seconds:	Level 3	15.04–17.43 seconds:	Level 3
16.84–19.30 seconds:	Level 2	17.44–19.81 seconds:	Level 2
19.31–999.00 seconds:	Level 1	19.82–999.00 seconds:	Level 1

Reaction Shuttle

MEN		WOMEN	
0.00–2.88 seconds:	Level 7	0.00–3.21 seconds:	Level 7
2.89–3.18 seconds:	Level 6	3.22–3.54 seconds:	Level 6
3.19–3.72 seconds:	Level 5	3.55–4.27 seconds:	Level 5
3.73–4.12 seconds:	Level 4	4.28–4.87 seconds:	Level 4
4.13–5.46 seconds:	Level 3	4.88–6.21 seconds:	Level 3
5.47–6.79 seconds:	Level 2	6.22–7.55 seconds:	Level 2
6.80–999.00 seconds:	Level 1	7.56–999.00 seconds:	Level 1

Standing Broad Jump

MEN		WOMEN	
114.00–999.00 inches:	Level 7	95.75–999.00 inches:	Level 7
101.25–113.75 inches:	Level 6	83.25–95.50 inches:	Level 6
64.25–101.00 inches:	Level 5	52.25–83.00 inches:	Level 5
39.00–64.00 inches:	Level 4	27.25–52.00 inches:	Level 4
26.50–38.75 inches:	Level 3	14.25–27.00 inches:	Level 3
14.50–26.25 inches:	Level 2	5.00–14.00 inches:	Level 2
0.00–14.25 inches:	Level 1	0.00–4.75 inches:	Level 1

Power Core

MEN		WOMEN	
0.00–20.00 seconds:	Level 7	0.00–17.99 seconds:	Level 7
20.01–27.31 seconds:	Level 6	18.00–24.50 seconds:	Level 6
27.32–36.45 seconds:	Level 5	24.51–32.93 seconds:	Level 5
36.46–43.55 seconds:	Level 4	32.94–39.44 seconds:	Level 4
43.56–48.72 seconds:	Level 3	39.45–42.07 seconds:	Level 3
48.73–53.73 seconds:	Level 2	42.08–44.65 seconds:	Level 2
53.74–999.00 seconds:	Level 1	44.66–999.00 seconds:	Level 1

Modified Power Core

MEN		WOMEN	
0.00–15.00 seconds:	Level 7	0.00–13.49 seconds:	Level 7
15.01–20.48 seconds:	Level 6	13.50–18.38 seconds:	Level 6
20.49–27.34 seconds:	Level 5	18.38–24.70 seconds:	Level 5

MEN		WOMEN	
27.34–32.66 seconds:	Level 4	24.70–29.58 seconds:	Level 4
32.67–36.54 seconds:	Level 3	29.59–31.56 seconds:	Level 3
36.55–40.30 seconds:	Level 2	31.56–33.49 seconds:	Level 2
40.30–999.00 seconds:	Level 1	33.49–999.00 seconds:	Level 1

Pickleball Sprint

MEN		WOMEN	
0.00–1.96 seconds:	Level 7	0.00–2.11 seconds:	Level 7
1.97–2.11 seconds:	Level 6	2.12–2.22 seconds:	Level 6
2.12–2.43 seconds:	Level 5	2.23–2.53 seconds:	Level 5
2.44–2.62 seconds:	Level 4	2.54–2.76 seconds:	Level 4
2.63–3.48 seconds:	Level 3	2.77–3.59 seconds:	Level 3
3.49–4.30 seconds:	Level 2	3.60–4.43 seconds:	Level 2
4.31–999.00 seconds:	Level 1	4.44–999.00 seconds:	Level 1

NEXT STEPS

For the purposes of this book, we have developed a system of levels to help better understand your results. Your results correlate to a given level for each test (Level 1 through 7). Statistically, you will probably score at different levels on some of the tests. In other words, you have strengths and weaknesses. In our long history of testing, very few individuals initially test at the same level in all five performance parameters. Most athletes have a proverbial Achilles' heel. This is good information to know as you begin all the components of PB-150.

LEVELING UP

One long-term goal is to have all five testing areas at the same level or very close. This does not mean you should pull back on a testing area so other areas can catch up. If your linear speed (sprint test) is a Level 4 and your other tests are a Level 3, don't stop trying to get your sprint time faster. Keep pushing for Level 5 with your sprint while you are working to get the other test results to Level 4. PB-150 will guide you through this process. Enjoy the process and the rewards as you level up.

HOW TO FIND YOUR LEVEL

Leveling up gives you your cumulative score. To find your complete pickleball score, add up all your levels. Here's the method:

Four-Way Agility: Level 3.
Reaction Shuttle: Level 3.
Standing Broad Jump: Level 3.
Power Core: Level 4.
Pickleball Sprint: Level 5.

You then add 3 + 3 + 3 + 4 + 5 = 18 for your leveling-up score. Now you can plug these into the categories below.

FIND YOUR LEVEL

31–35 = COMBINE CHAMPION—IN THE 95 PERCENT RANGE

This is a very high level of athleticism. This pickler could be a former college or pro athlete who has taken up pickleball, or an individual who has dedicated time to developing his or her athleticism. To be honest, this person is a bit of an athletic outlier, the equivalent to a top-ranked tennis player or an elite athlete in their prime. Please remember enjoyment and success of the game is best determined by your pickleball skills.

26–30 = HIGH-LEVEL ATHLETE
(POSSIBLY ASPIRING TO PLAY AT THE PROFESSIONAL LEVEL)—
IN THE 75 TO 85 PERCENT RANGE

This is someone who has most likely played sports and/or trained at a high level. Just like the combine champion, to achieve this level, the pickler has to score well in all five tests.

21–25 = COMPETITIVE PERFORMER

This is the serious pickler who plays at tournaments and wants to up their Dynamic Universal Pickleball Rating (DUPR) rating.

16–20 = COMMITTED RECREATION PLAYER

This is the sweet spot of the pickleball world. There's nothing the matter with staying at this range, especially if you're staying injury-free and having fun. If you are forty or older, this is a great leveling-up goal. This total allows you to perform all the necessary physical components to enjoy the game. If this pickler wants to put in a little extra training time, they are capable of making the leap to the next level.

11–15 = CONSISTENT PICKLEBALL PLAYER

This pickler may be a younger person who is just starting to develop some movement literacy and strength, or someone fifty-five plus who has been active but needs a little something extra to improve their game.

5–10 = TRUE BEGINNER OR A RESTART (SOMEONE WHO HAS BEEN INACTIVE FOR SIX MONTHS OR MORE)

Picklers in this category are smart. They want to stay injury-free and have fun, so they're being proactive from the start. These picklers may be rehabbing from an injury or have some long-term issues. Don't worry: the testing will give you some information that can help you with your style of play and strategy, thus enhancing your enjoyment of the game.

Now the adventure begins. You have turned on your GPS, and PB-150 is your route to improvement. You have laid the foundation with a successful PB combine.

PART 2

The Program

INTRODUCTION TO PB-150

Let's take a tour of the program. This program requires 150 minutes a week of training and covers all seven training components (as outlined in chapter one). We've designed PB-150 to give you both structure and freedom, to allow you to adapt and adjust to all the challenges and pleasures life will send your way. Our only caveat is this: it's important to allot some time to work out even if you're under stress. Even during a tough week, if possible, you'll want to do each of the components. Foam rolling and doing a dynamic warm-up during a family visit could be a lifesaver, especially as you lean over to pick up the new baby off the floor or sneak in an extra-competitive game of pickleball when your brother comes to town.

There may also be weeks when you can do more. For example, you might spend extra time on a move from your prehab routine to prevent injuries. Or you might add the sports vision training. And of course a little foam rolling might be in order every day to keep your fascia healthy.

These are examples of upgrading or adding to your workout cart or removing a workout item to lighten the load. As you get into the routine, you will find ways that you want to customize to fit your needs.

You need to maintain a balance by getting enough sleep and eating a healthy diet, including potential supplements and a healthy daily smoothie. There's an art to finding the middle ground between extremes, a tradition that ranges from Aristotle's golden mean to Goldilocks's conundrum. You're trying to figure out what's "just right."

Quick Tour of Workout PB-150: Requirements for the Week

1. Prehab: 2 sessions (10 minutes each) = 20 minutes.
2. Dynamic Warm-up: 2 sessions (10 minutes each) = 20 minutes.
3. Strength Training: 2 Sessions (20 minutes each) = 40 minutes.
4. Conditioning Drills: 2 Sessions (10 minutes each) = 20 minutes.

5. Core Work: 2 Sessions (10 minutes each) = 20 minutes.
6. Cooldown: 4 Sessions (5 minutes each) = 20 minutes.
7. Foam Rolling: 1 Session = 10 minutes.

THE PB-150 SET ROUTINE

A FIVE-DAY TEMPLATE

Below is a sample week of training to give you a feel for how the program works.

In this model sequence, Day 1 is primarily a strength day, and Day 2 is primarily a movement day. And on your off day, at least once a week, you foam roll.

Day 1 Workout: 35 minutes to complete
Prehab routine: Start on page 63.
Strength training: Start on page 87.
Cooldown: Start on page 134.

Day 2 Workout: 35 minutes to complete
Dynamic warm-up.
Conditioning drills.
Core work.
Cooldown.

Recovery Day
Foam roll 10 minutes.

Day 3
Repeat Day 1.

Day 4
Repeat Day 2.

A WALK-THROUGH: THE ELITE TRAINING CENTER MODEL

With this overview in mind, let's take a more interactive walk-through of PB-150. First, let us explain what we mean when we say *elite training facilities*, a term we use with great respect. These are well-equipped training centers with a strong leader and a comprehensive team who helps athletes progress physically and stay healthy. We've spent years working with many of these top-flight performance centers in different capacities.

These training centers use the most effective, evidence-based exercise methods and explore new and innovative ways to train athletes. We are constantly learning from the visionaries who create these training modules, which represent what we consider to be the gold standard.

THE COMPONENTS

With this in mind, let's take another look at the workout components that will make up your program, along with some further explanations. Our first stop on the tour of this Pickleball Sports Performance Training Center is the strength component.

THE STRENGTH COMPONENT

We aim to keep your training choices simple, yet offer options: body weight, dumbbells, kettlebells, and bands. Many of you will need weights that are heavier than fifteen pounds and a solid bench for the chest press. If you go to a gym, you're all set.

Also, this component will call for you to enlist your type A side to keep track of the program's three phases:

The general preparation phase.
The strength and size phase.
The power and speed phase.

PREHAB, DYNAMIC WARM-UP, CORE, COOLDOWN, AND FOAM ROLLING

The prehab, dynamic warm-up, core, foam rolling, and cooldown routines are designed to provide a foundation. Like yoga and Pilates, they offer a sequence of basic exercises that you master and use for the long term. If, after you master the moves, you feel you want more advanced routines, they are offered on the book's website.

DRILLS

This module prescribes fundamental movement drills that performance coaches have tested over time. We chose drills designed to help you move better globally (in all your activities) as well as on the pickleball court. The drills will have you move in all directions, improving your agility, balance, coordination, speed, and power. Some of the drills will have simple logical progressions that add complexity.

A COACHING STRATEGY

Here's one way to navigate this program: before you do the training section for that day, read the component chapters. For example, to prepare for the Day 1 workout, read the prehab, strength, and cooldown chapters. If you're having difficulty with an exercise, review the movement description and the coaching tips in the appropriate chapter.

As you become more familiar with the exercises through repetition, you'll feel confident referring to the book less frequently. And then, almost magically, you'll find you won't need these pages anymore. In this process, you will have to become your own personal trainer. Your empowerment is our goal.

THE WELLNESS COMPONENTS

We don't want to pile it on, and changes usually happen a step at a time, but don't forget about your wellness components. What can you integrate from chapter 14, "Nourish," and chapter 15, "The Pickleball Mindset"? We encourage you to incorporate one element at a time.

PB-150: GOING WITH THE FLOW: REMIX, UPGRADE, LIGHTEN THE LOAD

Let's look at some examples of how you can adapt this workout during your week.

COMBINING WORKOUTS

One method to customize the components is combining Days 1 and 2 into one 70-minute workout and Days 3 and 4 into a second 70-minute workout. Then you could do one workout on Tuesdays and another workout Thursdays. You would take Monday off to recover from pickleball and take Friday off in preparation to play pickleball on Saturday and Sunday (if you're a weekend pickleball player).

CHOOSE YOUR DAYS ON AND OFF

You could alternate your days in a variety of ways, for example:

Day 1 on Monday

Day 2 on Tuesday

Day 3 on Thursday

Day 4 on Saturday

Foam role on Wednesday or Friday

The point is, you can move the components around in a variety of ways as long as you have forty-eight hours between your strength training days.

THE PUZZLE PIECE METHOD

Let's say that even during a week when you have more obligations than usual, you still don't want to miss your court time and let your pickleball community down. Here's a possible scenario:

- Before your game, you do a dynamic warm-up, and after playing, you do your strength training and a cooldown.
- The following day, you have time for your prehab routine and core work.

- The next playing day, you repeat your dynamic warm-up, and postgame, you do your strength work, followed by a cooldown session.
- As the week finally gets less hectic, you look at the remaining requirements for the week. You do a foam rolling session; it feels really good and releases some tension. But you're tired, and you think of the other elements of a holistic program: sleep and nutrition. You eat a good meal, take the opportunity to do some vision training, and then go to bed early.
- As the week winds down, you get in another prehab, strength session, and conditioning drills.

Oh my god, you didn't get in two drills/conditioning sessions. You are in trouble; the pickleball fitness police will be paying you a visit. Actually . . .

Congratulations, you may not have hit every requirement for the week, but you trained smart, used the training principles, and made wise choices. You integrated two wellness elements; the only component you missed was one drills/conditioning session. You knew this was a wise choice.

The takeaway is that these components are like puzzle pieces that can fit into the shape of your week. You can pull them apart and reassemble them to work with your schedule.

MULTIPLE CONFIGURATIONS

Here are some criteria to think about putting together the puzzle of your workout week:

1. Try to plug in a dynamic warm-up, a prehab, or a foam roll around court time. All three can work before you play. A cooldown and a foam roll are also good post-playing. You could do a dynamic warm-up or prehab before playing and a cooldown or foam roll afterward. These are good ways to meet weekly requirements that support court time.

2. While still warmed up from playing, do your strength routine after your game. You could do the partner version right on the court.

3. Take at least one day off between strength days.

4. Do conditioning and drills before or after you play.

TO CONCLUDE

The main point: there are many ways you can piece together the PB-150 workout for your week. You can stick to the set plan—four workout days during the week and one foam rolling—or tweak it to fit your needs. For some of you, keeping the same routine works best. Others need a lot of flexibility, and still others need a little of both. With PB-150, all these options are available.

We designed the program to be holistic. This requires that you think holistically. How are you feeling? Did you get enough sleep? Have you eaten well today or in the last few days? Are you really stressed? Maybe you just need to do the pickleball dance warm-up, get on the court and have fun, then kick back and hydrate.

5.

PB-150 WORKOUT PLANNER

To give you a strong start in your PB-150 program, we'll guide you through the first three months. We break the program into three 4-week blocks followed by a transition period into Phase 2.

This overview provides the proper page number in each component chapter for your routines plus more detailed instructions on workout specifics. What does a typical day look like? A typical week? Keep reading for a helpful breakdown.

Daily Schedule: Minutes per Activity

DAY 1

Prehab, 10 minutes: page 63.

Strength, 20 minutes: page 87.

Cooldown, 5 minutes: page 134.

DAY 2

Dynamic warm-up, 10 minutes: page 73.

Drill/conditioning, 10 minutes: page 122.

Core, 10 minutes: page 103.

Cooldown, page 134.

SMARTER

SMART stands for Specific, Measurable, Achievable, Relevant, and Timebound. This goal-setting model was first developed by renowned management consultant Peter Drucker in the 1950s. Since then, Drucker's model has expanded beyond the management field. As trainers, we recommend using it as a thinking tool to help you plan and set your pickleball goals.

Specific: What are your clearly defined objectives? The PB-150 program's main goal is to make you a better pickleball player who is fitter, faster, stronger, more agile, and injury-resistant.

Measurable: What elements can you measure to track improvement, keep yourself motivated, and reveal what areas need to be adjusted? Our combined testing is designed for measurement. Your other measurables are lifting heavier weights, doing more reps, improving your balance during core work, and increasing your range of motion and your flexibility.

Achievable: What realistic short-term goals do you have? Trying to meet overly ambitious goals can leave you discouraged. Instead, the PB-150 program is balanced, so you have time to play pickleball, enjoy your life and fulfill your responsibilities, and engage in a holistic training program.

Relevant: Are your goals in line with your objectives? PB-150's design aligns with the book's vision—to make you a more athletic pickleball player and decrease your risk of injury.

Timebound: PB-150 is timebound in your daily, weekly, monthly, and long-term goals.

Exciting: Raise the stakes for achieving your goal in a fun way, so it's truly motivating. For example, if you follow the PB-150 Program faithfully for three months, maybe reward yourself with that new paddle you've been coveting. Or if you and your pickleball buddy stick with the program for six months, you travel to see one of the pro pickleball tournaments.

Record: This simply means write it down in some fashion. You can note your progress at the top of each week in your planner, type it in your notes app, or post it on your refrigerator.

DAY 3: RECOVERY DAY

Foam roll, 10 minutes: page 142.

DAY 4: REPEAT OF DAY 1

Prehab, 10 minutes: page 63.

Strength, 20 minutes: page 87.

Cooldown, 5 minutes: page 134.

DAY 5: REPEAT OF DAY 2

Dynamic warm-up, 10 minutes: page 73.

Drill/conditioning, 10 minutes: page 122.

Core, 10 minutes: page 103.

Cooldown, page 134.

Weekly Schedule: A Model of a Typical Week

Monday: Day 1

Tuesday: Day 2

Wednesday: Day 3: Recovery Day

Thursday: Day 4

Friday: Day 5

Saturday: Off Day

Sunday: Off Day

Guidelines

- Always take at least one day off between strength days. In this example, you have two strength training days off between Day 1 and Day 4. From Day 4 to the start of your new week equals three days between strength sessions. In general, the range of rest time between strength training sessions can be between 24 and 96 hours.

- Likewise, you have either two or three rest days between your core and conditioning days.

- As a general rule, optimal recovery time for strength, conditioning, and core sessions falls between 2 and 3 days.

Feel free to shift these rest days around to fit your personal schedule (but follow the rest guidelines). In the last chapter, we also discussed ways to customize the workout. To tailor the above template, if you have extra time, you could do a foam rolling session on the weekend. You will naturally fall into the best schedule for you.

THE FIRST THREE MONTHS: WHAT TO EXPECT

MONTH 1

Aim to build a solid foundation. You will learn how to do the exercises correctly, create a workout habit, and increase your work capacity.

MONTH 2

Continue to build your muscle strength and gain a higher level of mastery of the exercises. You may have noticed some quick gains that happened in Month 1 when you had no place to go but up. If your progress slows down, you might feel frustrated. Instead, celebrate the progress you've already made.

MONTH 3

Build a deep focus, feeling your muscles work with precision and power. Be on guard; you might zone out now that you are familiar with the routine. It's important to stay mindful of your muscle movements.

TRANSITION PERIOD

Take a week or two off to return stronger and refreshed.

The transition period is about recharging and resting, physically and mentally. You

THE ESSENTIAL STEPS TO MASTERY

Surrender to your passion (it's never too late). Find what captivates and inspires you, what you are willing to commit to for the long run.

Practice. Dedicate time to consistent practice. Mastery requires persistent effort over an extended period.

Love the plateau. Embrace periods of stagnation and plateaus in which progress seems slow or nonexistent.

Find a coach (a guide, mentor, or teacher). Get advice and help so you prevent time-consuming mistakes.

Become your own coach. For us, finding a coach or a mentor is excellent advice, and this can be transformative. But the greatest moments of mastery can also be when you're alone, no one's looking over your shoulder, and you're completely autonomous. This can be in your backyard, a converted garage space, the basement, or the living room after everyone's gone to bed. You're correcting, adjusting, and working through an exercise move, a drill, or a game skill, and you have an epiphany. There is no one cueing you. You've gained the ability to analyze and make adjustments on your own. It's not as if you'll never need help or coaching again. Even the greatest ones need that, but you've developed a practice where you are comfortable and confident enough to be a teacher and learner simultaneously. We call this caring and not caring. The caring is in the preparation, and the not caring is letting it fly.

Visualize an outcome. Part of the pleasure is the dreaming, so imagine, envision, conjure.

Play the edge. Test your boundaries with playfulness.

Maintain consistency. The old saying that "90 percent of life is showing up" is true, so keep showing up and practicing even when your motivation dips low.

Value the journey over the destination. Focus on the joy of learning and the process of improvement rather than solely fixating on the end goal.

Stay open to learning. Remain humble and open-minded throughout your journey. A true master never stops learning and growing.

This work was inspired by George Leonard.

can think of it as a two-week vacation. This doesn't mean you're inactive, but you do drop your training activity by 50 percent to give yourself a chance to recharge and enter the next three-month training cycle fully recovered. You will not lose any of your gains with this break. In fact, it will enable you to make more gains in your next training cycle.

During these two weeks, get a little extra sleep and eat healthy meals. For your activities and workouts, make choices that use different movement patterns:

- Take a 20- or 30-minute bike ride a couple of times a week.
- Join a yoga or Pilates class.
- Go bowling.
- Take hikes or walks in the park.

IN CONCLUSION

The goal of PB-150 is to introduce you to the major components of a complete sports fitness training program, improving your strength, power, speed, agility, and balance while lowering your risk of injury. The program is designed to accomplish this ambitious goal in the minimum amount of time. This gives you a framework for components you may want to explore in more depth.

MIND IN THE MUSCLE

A classic weight training motto: Put your mind in your muscle to build the mind-muscle connection; don't just go through the motions as your mind drifts. Arnold Schwarzenegger popularized this mind-body approach to strength training. In fact, Arnold sees the mind as the most essential part of training. The formal term for this, *internal attentional focus*, refers to tuning into what's happening in your body. Studies have demonstrated the benefits of attention directed to a specific muscle during an exercise. Researchers found that participants who focused on the target muscle during exercises exhibited significantly greater muscle activation than those who did not. This suggests that consciously directing attention to the working muscle can enhance muscle recruitment and the overall training effect. Mindfulness, which we hear about in yoga class, is clearly effective for strength training.

Approach becoming more mindful as a skill you can develop. You simply concentrate on feeling your working muscle go through its full range of motion.

Your focused attention can be critical to overcoming plateaus. We understand that no one has perfect attention, and we all get distracted. So when your mind wanders, return your focus to your workout. You'll be happy with the results.

PART 3

The Pickleball Training Components

6.

PREHAB

AN INJURY EPIDEMIC

Pickleball injuries are common and can be severe, preventing picklers from stepping onto the court and playing the game they love. Medical injury costs for pickleball in 2023 are predicted to be nearly $400 million. Healthcare visits in 2023 are estimated at 67,000 emergency department visits, 366,000 outpatient visits, 8,800 outpatient surgeries, 4,700 hospitalizations, and 20,000 post-acute episodes.

PICKLEBALL PREHAB

In the sports world, prehab is emerging as an essential part of staying injury-free and of increasing a player's longevity in a favorite sport. Traditionally, prehab was thought of as exercises you do before surgery. But it's since broken out of that box. Visionaries like the team at the Prehab Guys (the group also includes a number of women) have made it their mission to spread the power of prehab to the recreational athlete.

Your coach for this component is Arash Maghsoodi, a prehab pickleball specialist. He is the cofounder of the Prehab Guys. His journey as a performance physical therapist started after he sustained a career-ending ankle injury while playing collegiate soccer at San Diego State University. His experience of how life-altering injuries can be led to his choice to get his doctorate in physical therapy at USC. As an undergraduate, he studied kinesiology, the study of the mechanics of human movement, so he was already obsessed with human movement and performance. His injury also gave have him a passion for developing the concept of prehab—what you can do to prevent or minimize injuries before they happen.

MOBILITY AND STABILITY

Pickleball requires a wide range of motion in the ankles, knees, hips, shoulders, and elbows, along with spinal engagement for dinks and rotational power. The game also demands stability in all these joints. Mobility and stability are key themes throughout this book. Both are top of mind for experts in the sports training and physical therapy fields. Trainers and physical therapists know the importance of restoring and/or creating a fully functional combination of mobility (range of motion) and stability (strength) in your joints.

MAGHSOODI

The goal of the pickleball prehab routine is to create mobility and stability in the joints, while also restoring symmetry in the body as a whole. Lack of balance in the joints is known as asymmetry. Asymmetries develop naturally in response to your daily activities, any injuries you incur, and the sports you play. With pickleball you can develop an asymmetry because of how you use your dominant-side paddle arm.

Like all the components in this book, prehab helps you build a deep relationship with your body. When you go through your pickleball prehab routine, be mindful of how your joints move on both sides of your body. For example, do you have the same mobility and stability in both ankles? How about in your left and right hip? Notice whether one side lacks stability or the necessary strength to hold its position. Does one hip or joint have a limited range of motion? If so, give these areas a little extra attention. Body awareness is all part of your pickleball quest to know thyself.

SYNERGY OF PB-150

Designed for pickleball players of all levels and ages, your prehab routine includes exercises for each joint and key moves for spinal health. The routine works by isolating an area, giving it some prehab love to strengthen and improve mobility.

With PB-150, all components are linked together, making it a synergistic process. During strength training, the body performs multi-joint movements under load, strengthening all the major muscles and creating stability. In turn, this local strength helps you balance when doing the dynamic warm-up.

The next step is to dive into the routine. Here are some tips for getting the most out of it.

PREHAB GUYS PICKLEBALL ROUTINE

This routine is designed to work from the ground up, starting with your feet and moving to your neck. In a unique collaboration, the exercises in this routine will be presented in a series of videos to take you through the prehab process step by step. The exercise links will be on the home page of the book's website.

SINGLE-LEG HEEL LIFT—BIG TOE EXTENSION
2 SETS, 10 SECONDS, 2 × A WEEK

HOW: Place a folded towel on the ground. Stand near the towel with just your right big toe on it. Hold on to the wall or some other object for balance. Bend the left knee, bringing the left foot up off the ground. Press into the towel with the right big toe and lift your right heel slowly. Then return to the starting position. Repeat with the left toe on the towel.

FEEL: You should feel your calf working and a stretch in your big toe.

TRAINING TIP: Make sure only your big toe is on the towel.

🏓 HALF-KNEELING SOLEUS (CALF) STRETCH

2 SETS, 30 SECONDS HOLD, 3 × A WEEK

HOW: From a standing position, bend your left knee at 90 degrees and kneel on your right knee. With both hands on your left thigh, lean forward so that your left knee moves forward, past your toes. Maintaining that position, lift your left heel off the ground. Hold the forward lean position for the prescribed time or until you feel a good stretch in your left calf.

FEEL: You should feel a stretch in your calf, Achilles tendon, and toe flexors.

TRAINING TIPS: Make sure the heel lifts off the ground, but not so much that you don't feel a stretch in your calf.

You can put a towel under your knee for comfort.

🏓 QUADRUPED THREAD THE NEEDLE TO OPEN BOOK

2 SETS, 5 REPS ON EACH SIDE, 2 × A WEEK

HOW: Get down on all fours with your hands under your shoulders and your knees under your hips. Slowly lower your right shoulder and rotate your torso down and to your left, threading your right arm under your body and through to the other side. Then rotate up, raising your right shoulder, bringing your right hand behind your ear, and raising your elbow up to the sky. Follow the movement with your eyes.

FEEL: You should feel a nice and gentle rotational stretch in the middle of your back as you thread the needle, turning your body down and toward your opposite arm, then rotating your body up and out.

TRAINING TIP: Think of the name of the move, "threading the needle and opening the book." Keep your hips over your knees. Or sink your hips back toward your ankles. Do not let your hips come forward.

SINGLE LEG BRIDGE: LEG BENT

2 SETS, 10 REPS ON EACH SIDE, 2 × A WEEK

HOW: Lie on your back. Your left leg is bent at the knee, your left foot is flat on the floor, arms at your sides. Raise and bend your right leg toward your chest. Engaging your core, drive your left heel into the ground, lifting your left hip up toward the ceiling. At the end position, your left knee, hip, and shoulder should be in one straight line. Hold the end position, squeeze the glutes, then slowly return to starting position.

FEEL: You should feel your glutes work to control this motion. At no point should you feel your low back muscles doing the lifting motion. If you feel it only in your hamstrings, try bending your knee a bit more on the driving leg.

TRAINING TIP: Avoid arching the low back.

PRONE OVERHEAD PRESS

2 SETS, 10 REPS EACH, 2 × A WEEK

HOW: Lie face down, with your forehead resting on a towel and your arms positioned like goalposts out to your sides. Lift both arms together toward the ceiling, making sure to pull your shoulder blades together. Then reach both hands overhead, attempting to bring your biceps up toward your ears. Point the thumbs toward the ceiling as you reach overhead. Move slowly and controlled with this exercise.

MODIFICATION: If this is too difficult for you, you can do this one arm at a time or perform it off an elevated surface like a bed or table.

FEEL: The muscles around the shoulder blades and in the shoulders will be working with this exercise.

TRAINING TIP: Avoid arching the low back or shrugging the shoulder blades as you bring your arms overhead.

🏓 PRONE HIP EXTENSION

2 SETS, 10 REPS ON EACH SIDE, 2 × A WEEK

HOW: Lie face down with your legs straight and toes pushing into the ground. Fold your arms above your shoulders, and rest your forehead on your forearms. Engage your core and keep your knee straight as you lift one leg as high as you can without using your low back.

FEEL: Focus on feeling your hamstring and glute muscles working.

TRAINING TIP: Don't bend your knee when lifting your leg. Don't use your low back or twist it.

🏓 PRONE W WITH HEAD LIFT

2 SETS, 10 REPS, 2 X A WEEK

HOW: Lie face down with your arms out to the sides; bend your elbows to create the shape of a W. Tuck your chin slightly and lift your head off the floor while still looking down. Then lift only your upper back (not your lower back). With your upper back lifted, squeeze your shoulder blades together by lifting your elbows toward the ceiling, maintaining the W shape. Initiate the motion from between the shoulder blades, elevating the shoulders as high they can go. Return to the starting position.

FEEL: You should feel the muscles in your upper back, your neck, and your shoulder area (including between the shoulder blades) working.

TRAINING TIP: Avoid arching the low back; lift only your upper back. Don't let your chest lower as you go through your reps. Don't shrug the shoulder blades as you bring your arms overhead.

🏓 WRIST EXTENSOR STRETCH—DYNAMIC

2 SETS, 10 REPS EACH, 2 × A WEEK

HOW: Grasp the back of your left hand with the right, keeping your elbows slightly bent. Pull the left hand downward, keeping your left palm facing your body. At the same time, straighten your left elbow and begin to push the thumb side of your left hand outward, creating a stretch in the back of your left forearm. Hold that for the prescribed time. Repeat with the left hand grasping the right.

FEEL: You should feel a stretch in the back of the forearm that you are pulling down.

TRAINING TIPS: Don't straighten your elbow right away. Make sure to pull down and out on your wrist as you straighten the arm.

REVERSE SALAMANDER
2 SETS, 10 REPS EACH, 2 × A WEEK

HOW: Start face down on the floor, propped up on your forearms, and your knees under your hips. Drop the right hip and extend the right leg out behind you, placing the outside of the right foot on the ground. Press the right hip toward the floor. Bring the right leg in and repeat this movement with the left leg. Perform this exercise with your feet supported on the ground. You can make this exercise harder by keeping the working leg elevated to allow yourself to make contact with the floor only with the hips.

FEEL: You should feel the core muscles working here.

TRAINING TIPS: Rotate just from the hips down. Keep your forearms stable on the ground.

SIDE-LYING CHIN TUCK—ROTATION
2 SETS, 8 TO 12 REPS, 2 × A WEEK

HOW: Lie on your right side, keeping your head and neck in line with your spine in a neutral position. Perform a chin tuck by pushing your head slightly back while imagining elongating your neck. From here, rotate your chin to one shoulder and then to the opposite side for 1 rep.

FEEL: You should feel your neck muscles working.

TRAINING TIP: Maintain the neutral spine position for the entire time you perform this exercise.

7.

DYNAMIC WARM-UP

MOVE IS LUBE

A dynamic warm-up can be a pickleball game changer. Studies show it can decrease your risk of injury by up to 30 percent. Beyond that, if you make warming up a regular habit, it will transform the way you move throughout the day and as you age.

CONTEXT IS EVERYTHING: TIMING AND PURPOSE

In the late 1990s, sports scientists began questioning the benefits of static stretching as opposed to dynamic stretching before working out or playing a sport. Static stretching is the reach-and-hold method—what you may typically associate with stretching. The classic example is the seated forward bend. From a seated position, keeping your legs straight, you bend forward and reach toward your toes, then hold your maximum reach for 20 to 60 seconds. This technique is used in many yoga classes and high school gyms.

Dynamic stretching, on the other hand, involves motion. You move your body through ranges of motion that focus on a joint or joints as they activate muscles. An example is the hurdle step for the hips (swinging the leg forward and backward). This move takes the hip joint through a range of motion, from flexion to extension, requiring both mobility and stability in the hip joint to move with precision. The good news is that unlike most other cultural hot topics, neither method has been demonized in this debate. Sports scientists have arrived at an optimized solution that includes both static and dynamic stretching.

The static vs. dynamic stretch debate found resolution in these distinctions: timing and purpose. You should warm up with dynamic stretching in preparation for strenuous activity. More specifically, your dynamic warm-up should support the demands and purpose of the activity you're about to enter. A dynamic warm-up for pickleball differs from one carried out before running a 10K, playing a round of golf, or riding a bike. However, at the end of a workout, static stretching is best. Since the body is already warm, static stretching allows for safe flexibility gains and helps the body cool down and relax. In chapter 11, we prescribe a static stretching cooldown routine.

THE DYNAMIC WARM-UP: BENEFITS

The dynamic warm-up offers a long list of benefits that go beyond pickleball. At a global, whole-body level, the dynamic warm-up will improve your balance, coordination, and strength. You'll obtain better mobility and stability in your joints. You will even develop better posture. Your dynamic warm-up increases your body's core temperature and activates your muscles. And because it causes synovial fluids to flow and then lubricate the joints, you're primed to play with a reduced risk of injury. The combination of increasing your body temperature and challenging your muscles with dynamic movements helps free your muscles. Any form of sitting, such as at work, at home, or in the car, stiffens muscles, making them "sticky." Dynamic movement increases muscle fluidity. Unlike static stretching, dynamic movement is effective even at a deep physiological level in and through the muscle spindles, opening the communication lines between your mind and your muscles. The result? You're ready for the moves and fast reactions that pickleball demands. Dynamic movement creates a fluid mind-body conversation that enables you to play with force and power—safely and efficiently.

Soon you may find yourself doing micro-dynamic stretches throughout the day to counter the wear and tear of regular life. You may be at a rest stop in the Rocky Mountains doing some moves beside your car. Occasionally, such actions may garner some strange looks. It's worth it.

GENERAL GUIDELINES: HOW LONG, HOW MANY, HOW TO

The design of the dynamic workout moves from simple and easy to more complex and challenging. Some pro athletes may spend as much as 20 to 30 minutes on a dynamic warm-up. Think of it as part of your workout, not something separate. Your pickleball warm-up routine will take about 10 minutes, with each movement sequence lasting between 15 and 30 seconds.

Proper technique for each movement is important, so spend a little time working on each exercise before adding reps. Ultimately, you can think of the routine as having a flow, like a dance.

The Workout

- Perform the dynamic warm-up exercises in a controlled manner, finding the pattern in the movement—its beginning, middle, and end.

- Think about your movement fundamentals when you do the routine: alignment, core activation, weight shift, center of gravity, application of body weight.

- Keep your movements controlled; avoid any jerky motions.

- Engage your core muscles to maintain balance and stability throughout the exercise.

- Do the dynamic warm-up before playing a match or before any strenuous activity.

- Always work in a pain-free range of motion.

- Find a flat and open space where you can move comfortably for 5 to 10 yards.

DYNAMIC WARM-UP PREP: ROLL OUT ALL YOUR JOINTS

ANKLE CIRCLES: 3 TO 5 CIRCLES IN EACH DIRECTION

Gently make small circles with your ankles—clockwise and counterclockwise.

KNEES AND HIPS

Knee Circles: 3 to 5 circles in each direction
Gently make small circles with your knees—clockwise and counterclockwise.

Hip Circles: 3 to 5 circles in each direction
Gently make small circles with your hips—clockwise and counterclockwise.

WRISTS AND SHOULDERS

Wrist Circles and Flex and Extend: 3 to 5 circles
Gently make small circles with your wrists—clockwise and counterclockwise.

Flex your wrists down (fingers pointing to the floor). Extend your wrists up (fingers pointing to the ceiling).

Shoulder Circles: 3 to 5 circles
Shrug your shoulders up toward your ears; then pull them down. Roll your shoulders up, forward, down, and back a few times; then reverse the direction of the roll.

ARM CIRCLES: 3 TO 5 CIRCLES

Stand with your feet shoulder width apart. Extend your arms, palms down, straight out to the sides, parallel to the ground.

Circle your arms forward, out in front of your body, then backward, going slightly behind your upper body.

Reverse the direction, circling your arms behind your body, then forward and back up.

NECK CIRCLES: 6 CIRCLES

Rotate your head clockwise and counterclockwise, reversing direction with each rotation. Think of drawing a circle with your nose. Do 3 rotations clockwise, and 3 counterclockwise.

- Listen to your body. Feel free to ease into the dynamic warm-up, modifying moves for comfort and shortening the duration of each move.

- Avoid excessive stretching or pulling.

THE ROUTINE:
ORDER OF PERFORMANCE

Walks

PHASE ONE: HEEL WALK

10 TO 20 STEPS

With your feet hip width apart, stand in good alignment: shoulders, hips, and knees in one line, with weight distributed evenly.

Lift your toes off the ground, so you're standing on your heels.

Press your heels into the ground. Keep your toes angled toward your shins. Walk forward on your heels. Start with small steps and gradually increase to your normal step length.

Concentrate on leading with your heels. Keep your toes pointing up toward your shins.

Maintain good posture throughout the exercise.

Continue walking forward for 10 to 20 steps.

TOE WALK

10 TO 20 STEPS

Stand in good alignment, with your feet hip width apart.

Raise both heels off the ground, shifting your body weight to the balls of your feet.

Begin walking forward slowly, keeping your heels off the ground the entire time.

Keep your gaze forward, looking in front of you, not down at your toes.

Continue walking forward for 10 to 20 steps.

SIDE ANKLE WALK
10 TO 20 STEPS

Stand in good alignment, with your feet hip width apart.

Place your body weight on the outside edges of your feet.

Begin walking forward, but instead of rolling through your feet normally, focus on walking on the outer edges of your feet.

As you step forward, consciously place the outer edge of your heel first, and follow the outside edge of your foot to the little toe.

Continue walking forward for 10 to 20 steps.

Maintain a slow and controlled pace as you continue walking, making sure to stay balanced and stable. This move helps prevent the most common ankle sprains—when the foot rolls to the outside—so don't let the foot roll out too far, overstressing the ankle.

HURDLE STEP
3 TO 5 STEPS WITH EACH LEG

Imagine you are stepping forward over a low hurdle, bringing your leg out to the side and over. Repeat in the opposite direction, as if you're stepping backward over a low hurdle.

Step over forward and backward with the same leg, then switch legs.

HUG AND RELEASE
3 TO 5 HUGS AND RELEASES

Stand in good alignment, with your feet hip width apart.

- **Hug:** Wrap your arms around your body and try to grasp the back of your opposing shoulder. Focus on feeling your shoulder blades slide apart toward the side of the ribs.

- **Release:** Spread your arms out wide in a W shape, bringing your shoulder blades close together.

SOS

3 TO 5 SOS'S

Stand in good alignment, with your feet hip width apart. Raise your arms above
your head.

Step to your right, shifting your body weight to the right leg. Stretch and lengthen
both arms in that direction.

Then shift your body weight to your left leg as your upper body and arms follow.

Increase the speed, shifting from left to right, as if you're shipwrecked on an island
and a rescue plane is in view.

Extra challenge: lift the left leg as you stretch right; lift the right leg as you stretch
left.

PHASE TWO: KNEE-TO-CHEST WALK

3 TO 5 STEPS WITH EACH LEG

Stand in good alignment, with your feet hip width apart.

Lift your right knee toward your chest, grasping it with both hands
just below the knee.

Gently pull your knee to your chest. Hold this position for a couple
of seconds.

Lower your leg back to the ground and step forward with your left
foot.

Repeat the same movement with your left leg, bringing your knee to
your chest.

Continue alternating between your right and left legs.

QUAD STRETCH

3 TO 5 STRETCHES OF EACH LEG

Stand in good alignment, with your feet hip width apart.

Balancing on your right foot, lift your left heel off the ground and grab your ankle with your left hand, then raise your right arm to the sky.

Gently pull your left foot toward your glutes, feeling a stretch in the front of your left thigh (quadriceps).

Maintain good posture by keeping your chest up and your core engaged.

Release the stretch, take a step forward with your left foot, and repeat the stretch on the right side.

FIGURE-4 SQUAT

3 TO 5 FIGURE-4 SQUATS ON EACH LEG

Stand upright with your feet hip width apart.

Take a step forward with your left foot. Keep your torso upright and engage your core muscles.

As you step forward, lift your right foot off the ground and cross it over your left leg. Place the outside of your right ankle just above your left knee (forming the shape of a figure 4).

Repeat the movement with the right foot stepping forward and the left foot crossing over the right, performing the figure-4 squat.

KNEE TOWARD OPPOSITE SHOULDER

3 TO 5 REPETITIONS ON EACH LEG

Balance on your left leg.

With both hands, grab your right knee and pull it across and up toward your left shoulder.

Be gentle but firm with the movement.

Repeat the movement with the left knee.

LUNGE WALK WITH ROTATION

3 TO 5 LUNGES

Stand in good alignment, with your feet hip width apart.

Take a step forward with your left foot in a lunging motion, bending both knees.

Lower your body until your left thigh is parallel to the ground or as close as you can get it pain-free.

As you lunge forward, simultaneously rotate your upper body to the left, toward the forward leg, moving from your middle back.

Keep your arms extended straight out in front of you as you rotate.

Rise back to the starting position and repeat the motion with your right leg.

Continue alternating legs and rotating your upper body as you lunge-walk forward.

BACKWARD LUNGE

HANDS OVERHEAD WITH SIDE BEND: 3 TO 5 LUNGES

Stand in good alignment, with your feet hip width apart.

Take a step backward with your right leg in a lunging motion, bending both knees.

Lower your body until your left thigh is parallel to the ground or as close as you can get it pain-free.

As you lunge backward, simultaneously raise both arms above your head, elbows at your ears, shoulders back and down, then side bend to your left away from the leg that stepped back.

Push off with your left foot and bring your left leg behind your right leg, reversing the position and side bending to your right.

Continue stepping backward, alternating legs, and side bending.

Aim for smooth and controlled movements, maintaining proper alignment with your upper body.

AIRPLANES

3 TO 5 REPS ON EACH LEG

Stand in good alignment, with your
feet hip width apart, hands at your
side.

Take a step forward with your left foot, then extend your
arms out to the sides, forming a T shape with your body.

Keeping your left foot in place, rotate your torso to the left
and reach your right hand toward your left foot. Your left
arm should be pointing straight out to the side.

Return to the starting position and bring your arms back to the sides, alternating
sides each time.

PHASE THREE: JOG FORWARD

30 SECONDS

Stand in good alignment, with your feet hip width apart.

Begin jogging in place, then gradually increase your pace and run forward.

Keep your pace moderate, allowing your body to warm up gradually.

Gradually pick up your pace.

JOG BACKWARD

15 TO 30 SECONDS

Stand in good alignment, with your feet hip width apart.

Jog backward at an easy pace, landing on the balls of your feet.

Engage your core and maintain an upright posture throughout the exercise.

🔖 BUTT KICKS
15 TO 30 SECONDS

Stand in good alignment, with your feet hip width apart.

Jog in place while kicking your heels up toward your glutes. This movement warms up the quadriceps and stretches the hip flexors.

🔖 LATERAL SHUFFLE
15 TO 30 SECONDS

Stand in good alignment, with your feet hip width apart.

Engage your core muscles and keep your back straight throughout the exercise.

Step to the side with your right foot, pushing off with your left foot.

As you land with your right foot, bring your left foot toward your right foot, shuffling laterally.

Repeat the lateral shuffle for several steps to the right.

Then shuffle to the left by stepping to the side with your left foot and bringing your right foot toward your left foot.

Focus on maintaining a quick and controlled movement, keeping your feet low to the ground.

🔖 JUMPING JACKS
30 SECONDS

🔖 CARIOCA
30 SECONDS

Stand in good alignment, with your feet hip width apart.

Step your left leg behind and across your right foot.

Next, step your right foot out to the side, then cross your left leg in front of your right leg.

Moving sideways, repeat this cross-step pattern, alternating the crossing the left leg behind and in front of your right leg.

Repeat in the opposite direction, stepping sideways with you left leg and crossing your right leg behind and in front as you move sideways.

As you become more comfortable with the movement, try to increase the speed, keeping the motion fluid and controlled.

SQUAT AND TOUCH THE SKY

3 TO 5 SQUAT REACHES

Stand in good alignment, with your feet hip width apart.

Squat down and touch the ground between your legs. Explode to the balls of your feet as you reach your hands up to the sky.

SKIP FORWARD

15 TO 30 SECONDS

Start with a marching motion, then break into skip after a few marches.

Jog or skip backward and repeat the forward skip.

LATERAL HOPS

15 TO 30 SECONDS

Hop from side to side, covering a distance that feels safe.

FAST FEET

15 TO 30 SECONDS

Standing in one place, quickly step your feet up and down as if you were on hot sand at the beach.

Jog, Run, Sprint

🏓 PICKLEBALL PANTOMIME

Visualize in your mind and pantomime some game motions with your paddle: dinks, volleys at the kitchen line, ground strokes, and serves. Feel these moves in your body.

IN CONCLUSION

Your dynamic warm-up will soon become a personal ritual. Be sure to make it your own. Adjust it to fit your daily needs. Some days you will have more or less time. And depending on your body, you may give additional time to some movements. As you develop a flow, you will feel the joy that comes with waking up your joints and muscles, then progressing to more challenging full-body movements like jogging, skipping, shuffling, and bouncing.

STRENGTH TRAINING

Strength training is a crucial part of fitness, equal to cardio training. Here's a quick list of benefits:

- Decreases muscle loss as you age.
- Increases bone strength and density.
- Boosts metabolism to maintain a healthy body composition (more muscle, less fat).
- Improves athletic markers: speed, power, agility, and balance.
- Reduces risk of chronic diseases.
- Improves mood, working against symptoms of depression.
- Enhances cognitive function.
- Helps increase the production of testosterone.

To achieve these results, this component uses a five-phase process to make you strong and improve your pickleball game. This process is based on the time-tested concept of periodization, the planned manipulation of training variables, which is a verified and proven method for building strength.

THE EFFORT SCALE

Effort exertion is hard to measure. We'll discuss fatigue and a breakdown in technique to understand what we'll call *intelligent effort*.

The first criterion for intelligent effort is a breakdown in technique. When you have a breakdown in proper training technique, the set is over—you stop. Continuing after a breakdown is called a cheat, a somewhat dramatic and perhaps negative way to describe an attempt to gain a biomechanical advantage to complete a repetition. Arching your back on a dumbbell bench press is an example of poor technique. This can increase your chances of injury. Here's a checklist for what constitutes a breakdown in technique:

- Losing proper setup and alignment for the exercise.
- Failing to complete a full range of motion.
- Losing the precision and control of the movement.
- Zoning out mentally.

INTELLIGENT EFFORT

An important tool for getting your brain and body wrapped around the concept of intelligent effort is using the rating of perceived exertion (or effort) scale (RPE) to examine the right level of effort in a set of exercise (or knowing when to stop the exercise, completing the set).

We'll use the RPE developed by Dr. Gunnar Borg (1927–2020), who was a professor of perception and psychophysics at Stockholm University. Borg compared participants' ratings on this scale with physiological measurements. By establishing correlations between perceived exertion and objective physiological markers, he demonstrated the validity and reliability of the RPE scale as a subjective measure of effort during physical activity.

We'll use a modified version of the RPE scale with a numerical rating from 1 to 10 (1 being the easiest, 10 being the hardest), adapted to strength training. Here's the scale with a description for each number.

1. Almost no effort to perform reps.
2. Very easy to perform reps.
3. Easy to perform reps.
4. Starting to feel the muscles working.
5. Moderate exertion, feeling increased muscle activity.
6. Experiencing light muscle fatigue.
7. Experiencing moderate muscle fatigue.
8. Experiencing heavy muscle fatigue: challenging to maintain good form.
9. Experiencing extreme muscle fatigue: very challenging to complete a rep.
10. Maximal exertion: Muscles have reached complete exhaustion.

Our recommendation is pushing yourself to a minimum RPE of 6 and aim for an RPE of 8. Pushing yourself to a 9 is admirable and will give you significant gains, but going to this level can increase your chances of injury and increase chances of overtraining and burnout. Ultimately, your training intensity is a personal choice depending on your goals and fitness level.

THE TAKEAWAY FOR PB-150

We suggest you focus on strict form and aim for an effort level between 6 and 8. Going beyond 80 percent effort increases your risk of injury without a substantial training benefit. Take a long view, be inspired to train the next day, and be ready for your next game of pickleball. Training at higher intensity levels is also mentally exhausting, can make you dread training, and hence can decrease the likelihood of your staying on the program.

There is another element to intelligent effort (IE), which is almost the exact opposite of artificial intelligence (AI). It involves being mindfully engaged with your body, tuning into how it feels. This tuning into how you feel, an inner awareness of body sensations—heartbeat, breathing, fatigue—is called interoception. Interoception is an important skill to develop. Focusing on your inner cues helps you decide if you have had enough. This is a question you also need to ask yourself on the pickleball court. Should I play another game or call it a day? Am I dehydrated? Does my Achilles tendon feel a little stiff? One goal of training is to increase your awareness of your body and have this carry over onto the court.

If you feel that you have progressed to an elite level and have been cleared by a doctor, then you could push to a 9.

STRUCTURE AND CHANGE

These two concepts, structure and change, have been the subject of a great fitness debate for years. The debate reached its height when the phrase *muscle confusion* came into the mainstream workout culture. To be effective, you don't want to confuse your muscles. Instead, you should develop them in a respectful way, creating a collaborative relationship between your fitness goals and your body's well-being. Strive for planned change, which is both an art and a science.

Muscle confusion can happen because the first adaptations to a movement or exercise are neurological. So when you perform a new exercise, you can lift more weight and do more repetitions in the early phase, not because the muscle has gotten stronger or bigger but because you've become more neurologically efficient at doing the exercise and can thus move more weight. The body first wants to master movement. If you switch up your workouts too often, especially if you are a beginner or if you're learning a new exercise, your body is primarily making neurological adaptations to master the movement, but you're not getting optimal muscle activation and growth.

Your preference for either structure or change is a reflection of your personality. Some people need a lot of change to keep them interested. Others like repetition with a set structure, like Pilates and most forms of yoga. PB-150 is designed for both types. Be sure to allow for proper rest time between workout days (page 17).

ONWARD

As you begin your routine, the two main points to focus on are the proper technique for each exercise and hitting a safe level of effort as outlined above. If you need to review any training principles, these are in chapter 2.

TWO-WEEK PREP PHASE

If you are a beginner or have taken a long break from lifting (six months to a year), this is a safe and effective way to start the program.

Guidelines

1. For each exercise, refer to the Exercise Library (part 5), where you'll find illustrations and a complete description.
2. Use a light weight.
3. Focus on technique and learning the exercise.
4. Stop well short of the number of repetitions you could do if you went to fatigue. You want to give your muscles and body a little taste of strength training to avoid soreness or potential injuries as you start on Phase 1.
5. Follow the set, rep, and rest time prescriptions for each exercise.
6. Keep track of your workouts in a training notebook.

Week 1

DAY 1
Squat: 1 × 8
Lunge: 1 × 8 each leg
Hinge: 1 × 8
Push: 1 × 8
Pull: 1 × 8
Press: 1 × 8
Auxiliary (Calf): 1 × 8 each leg
Auxiliary (Wrist Curl): 1 × 8

DAY 2
Squat: 1 × 8
Lunge: 1 × 8 each leg
Hinge: 1 × 8

Push: 1 × 8

Pull: 1 × 8

Press: 1 × 8

Auxiliary (Calf): 1 × 8 each leg

Auxiliary (Curl): 1 × 8

Auxiliary (Lateral Raise): 1 × 8

Week 2

DAY 1

Squat: 1 × 10

Lunge: 1 × 10 each leg

Hinge: 1 × 10

Push: 1 × 10

Pull: 1 × 10

Press: 1 × 10

Auxiliary (Calf): 1 × 12 each leg

Auxiliary (Wrist Curl): 1 × 10

DAY 2

Squat: 1 × 12

Lunge: 1 × 12 each leg

Hinge: 1 × 12

Push: 1 × 12

Pull: 1 × 12

Press: 1 × 12

Auxiliary (Calf): 1 × 15 each leg

Auxiliary (Curl): 1 × 12

Auxiliary (Lateral Raise): 1 × 12

THE WORKOUT: MONTH 1

This month is the general preparation phase. The goal of this phase is to introduce you to the routine, giving you a chance to learn the workout step by step, while building muscle, improving endurance, and strengthening connective tissue.

Guidelines

1. For each exercise, refer to the Exercise Library (part 5), where you'll find illustrations and a complete description.
2. Use a light weight.
3. Focus on technique and learning the exercise.
4. Follow the set, rep, and rest time prescriptions for each exercise.
5. Keep track of your workouts in a training notebook.

PB-150 PHASE 1

Week 1

Rest 30 seconds between exercises.

DAY 1

Squat: 1 × 15, 1 × 12
Lunge: 1 × 15 each leg
Hinge: 1 × 15, 1 × 12
Push: 1 × 15, 1 × 12
Pull: 1 × 15, 1 × 12
Press: 1 × 15, 1 × 12
Auxiliary (Calf): 1 × 20 each leg
Auxiliary (Lateral Raise): 1 × 15
Auxiliary (Curl): 1 × 15
Auxiliary (Wrist Curl): 1 × 15

DAY 2

Squat: 1 × 15, 1 × 12

Lunge: 1 × 15 each leg

Hinge: 1 × 15, 1 × 12

Push: 1 × 15, 1 × 12

Pull: 1 × 15, 1 × 12

Press: 1 × 15, 1 × 12

Auxiliary (Calf): 1 × 20 each leg

Auxiliary (Post Delt Raise): 1 × 15

Auxiliary (Curl): 1 × 15

Auxiliary (Reverse Wrist Curl): 1 × 15

Week 2

Rest 20 seconds between exercises.

DAY 1:

Squat: 1 × 15, 1 × 12

Lunge: 1 × 15 each leg, 1 × 12 each leg

Hinge: 1 × 15, 1 × 12

Push: 1 × 15, 1 × 12

Pull: 1 × 15, 1 × 12

Press: 1 × 15, 1 × 12

Auxiliary (Calf): 1 × 20 each leg

Auxiliary (Lateral Raise): 1 × 15

Auxiliary (Curl): 1 × 15

Auxiliary (Wrist Curl): 1 × 15

DAY 2

Squat: 1 × 15, 1 × 12

Lunge: 1 × 15 each leg, 1 × 12 each leg

Hinge: 1 × 15, 1 × 12

Push: 1 × 15, 1 × 12

Pull: 1 × 15, 1 × 12

Press: 1 × 15, 1 × 12

Auxiliary (Calf): 1 × 20 each leg

Auxiliary (Post Delt Raise): 1 × 15

Auxiliary (Curl): 1 × 15

Auxiliary (Rotation Wrist Curl): 1 × 15

Week 3

Rest 10 seconds between exercises.

DAY 1

Squat: 1 × 15, 1 × 12

Lunge: 1 × 15 each leg, 1 × 12 each leg

Hinge: 1 × 15, 1 × 12

Push: 1 × 15, 1 × 12

Pull: 1 × 15, 1 × 12

Press: 1 × 15, 1 × 12

Auxiliary (Calf): 1 × 20 each leg

Auxiliary (Lateral Raise): 1 × 15, 1 × 12

Auxiliary (Curl): 1 × 15

Auxiliary (Wrist Curl): 1 × 15

DAY 2

Squat: 1 × 15, 1 × 12

Lunge: 1 × 15 each leg, 1 × 12 each leg

Hinge: 1 × 15, 1 × 12

Push: 1 × 15, 1 × 12

Pull: 1 × 15, 1 × 12

Press: 1 × 15, 1 × 12

Auxiliary (Calf): 1 × 20 each leg

Auxiliary (Post Delt Raise): 1 × 15, 1 × 12

Auxiliary (Curl): 1 × 15

Auxiliary (Rotation Wrist Curl): 1 × 15

Week 4

Perform the first set of each exercise in the order provided without resting, rest 2 minutes, then perform the second set of all exercises required in the order provided.

DAY 1

Squat: 1 × 15, 1 × 12
Push: 1 × 15, 1 × 12
Lunge: 1 × 15 each leg, 1 × 12 each leg
Pull: 1 × 15, 1 × 12
Hinge: 1 × 15, 1 × 12
Press: 1 × 15, 1 × 12
Auxiliary (Calf): 1 × 20 each leg, 1 × 15 each leg
Auxiliary (Lateral Raise): 1 × 15, 1 × 15
Auxiliary (Post Delt Raise): 1 × 15, 1 × 15
Auxiliary (Wrist Curl): 1 × 15, 1 × 15

DAY 2

Squat: 1 × 15, 1 × 12
Push: 1 × 15, 1 × 12
Lunge: 1 × 15 each leg, 1 × 12 each leg
Pull: 1 × 15, 1 × 12
Hinge: 1 × 15, 1 × 12
Press: 1 × 15, 1 × 12
Auxiliary (Calf): 1 × 20 each leg, 1 × 15 each leg
Auxiliary (Lateral Raise): 1 × 15, 1 × 15
Auxiliary (Curl): 1 × 15, 1 × 15
Auxiliary (Rotation Wrist Curl): 1 × 15, 1 × 15

THE WORKOUT: MONTH 2

The goal of this stage is to build muscle size. We lower your reps (to the 8 to 12 range), so you'll be using heavier resistance. This will add size to your muscles and prepare you for the next phase, adding strength and power.

Follow the same general guidelines as Month 1.

PB-150 PHASE 2

Week 1

Rest 30 seconds between exercises.

DAY 1

Squat: 1 × 10, 1 × 8

Lunge: 1 × 10 each leg, 1 × 8 each leg

Hinge: 1 × 10, 1 × 8

Push: 1 × 10, 1 × 8

Pull: 1 × 10, 1 × 8

Press: 1 × 10, 1 × 8

Hinge to Upright Row to Push Press: 1 × 10

Auxiliary (Calf): 1 × 20 each leg

Auxiliary (Lateral Raise): 1 × 10, 1 × 8

Auxiliary (Curl): 1 × 10, 1 × 8

Auxiliary (Wrist Curl): 1 × 15

DAY 2

Squat: 1 × 10, 1 × 8

Lunge: 1 × 10 each leg

Hinge: 1 × 10, 1 × 8

Push: 1 × 10, 1 × 8

Pull: 1 × 10, 1 × 8

Press: 1 × 10, 1 × 8

Hinge to Upright Row to Push Press: 1 × 10

Auxiliary (Calf): 1 × 20 each leg

Auxiliary (Post Delt Raise): 1 × 10, 1 × 8

Auxiliary (Curl): 1 × 10, 1 × 8

Auxiliary (Reverse Wrist Curl): 1 × 15

Week 2

Rest 25 seconds between exercises.

DAY 1

Squat: 1 × 10, 1 × 8, 1 × 7

Lunge: 1 × 10 each leg, 1 × 8 each leg

Hinge: 1 × 10, 1 × 8, 1 × 7

Push: 1 × 10, 1 × 8

Pull: 1 × 10, 1 × 8

Press: 1 × 10, 1 × 8

Hinge to Upright Row to Push Press: 1 × 10

Auxiliary (Calf): 1 × 20 each leg

Auxiliary (Lateral Raise): 1 × 10, 1 × 8

Auxiliary (Curl): 1 × 10, 1 × 8

Auxiliary (Wrist Curl): 1 × 15

DAY 2

Squat: 1 × 10, 1 × 8

Lunge: 1 × 10 each leg

Hinge: 1 × 10, 1 × 8

Push: 1 × 10, 1 × 8, 1 × 7

Pull: 1 × 10, 1 × 8, 1 × 7

Press: 1 × 10, 1 × 8

Hinge to Upright Row to Push Press: 1 × 10

Auxiliary (Calf): 1 × 20 each leg

Auxiliary (Post Delt Raise): 1 × 10, 1 × 8

Auxiliary (Curl): 1 × 10, 1 × 8

Auxiliary (Reverse Wrist Curl): 1 × 15

Week 3

Rest 20 seconds between exercises.

DAY 1

Squat: 1 × 10, 1 × 8, 1 × 7

Lunge: 1 × 10 each leg, 1 × 8 each leg

Hinge: 1 × 10, 1 × 8, 1 × 7

Push: 1 × 10, 1 × 8

Pull: 1 × 10, 1 × 8

Press: 1 × 10, 1 × 8, 1 × 7

Hinge to Upright Row to Push Press: 1 × 10

Auxiliary (Calf): 1 × 20 each leg

Auxiliary (Lateral Raise): 1 × 10, 1 × 8

Auxiliary (Curl): 1 × 10, 1 × 8

Auxiliary (Wrist Curl): 1 × 15

DAY 2

Squat: 1 × 10, 1 × 8

Lunge: 1 × 10 each leg

Hinge: 1 × 10, 1 × 8

Push: 1 × 10, 1 × 8, 1 × 7

Pull: 1 × 10, 1 × 8, 1 × 7

Press: 1 × 10, 1 × 8, 1 × 7

Hinge to Upright Row to Push Press: 1 × 10

Auxiliary (Calf): 1 × 20 each leg

Auxiliary (Post Delt Raise): 1 × 10, 1 × 8

Auxiliary (Curl): 1 × 10, 1 × 8

Auxiliary (Reverse Wrist Curl): 1 × 15

Week 4

Rest 15 seconds between exercises.

DAY 1:

Squat: 1 × 10, 1 × 8, 1 × 7

Lunge: 1 × 10 each leg, 1 × 8 each leg

Hinge: 1 × 10, 1 × 8, 1 × 7

Push: 1 × 10, 1 × 8, 1 × 7

Pull: 1 × 10, 1 × 8, 1 × 7

Press: 1 × 10, 1 × 8, 1 × 7

Hinge to Upright Row to Push Press: 1 × 8

Auxiliary (Calf): 1 × 20 each leg

Auxiliary (Lateral Raise): 1 × 10, 1 × 8

Auxiliary (Curl): 1 × 10, 1 × 8

Auxiliary (Wrist Curl): 1 × 15

DAY 2

Squat: 1 × 10, 1 × 8

Lunge: 1 × 10 each leg

Hinge: 1 × 10, 1 × 8

Push: 1 × 10, 1 × 8, 1 × 7

Pull: 1 × 10, 1 × 8, 1 × 7

Press: 1 × 10, 1 × 8, 1 × 7

Hinge to Upright Row to Push Press: 1 × 8

Auxiliary (Calf): 1 × 20 each leg

Auxiliary (Post Delt Raise): 1 × 10, 1 × 8

Auxiliary (Curl): 1 × 10, 1 × 8

Auxiliary (Reverse Wrist Curl): 1 × 15

THE WORKOUT: MONTH 3

STRENGTH PHASE

Now your body is ready to handle heavy weight that will allow you to perform between 4 to 6 reps. Heavier weight increases the intensity of these workouts. In this stage, you're getting stronger, so you can convert that strength to power in the next phase. If you're just doing body weight, you need to choose a more difficult exercise for each movement pattern. For example, for push-ups, a slide push-up, or for squats, a single-leg squat.

Follow the same general guidelines as the previous month.

PB-150 PHASE 3

Week 1

Rest 45 seconds between exercises.

DAY 1

Squat: 1 × 6, 1 × 5, 1 × 4
Lunge: 1 × 6 each leg, 1 × 5 each leg
Hinge: 1 × 6, 1 × 5, 1 × 4
Push: 1 × 6, 1 × 5, 1 × 4
Pull: 1 × 6, 1 × 5
Press: 1 × 6, 1 × 5
Rotation Snatch: 1 × 3 speed
Auxiliary (Calf): 1 × 20 each leg
Auxiliary (Lateral Raise): 1 × 10
Auxiliary (Curl): 1 × 10

DAY 2

Perform with a light weight and emphasize speed of movement, keeping good
   technique.
Squat: 1 × 6, 1 × 5, 1 × 4
Lunge: 1 × 6 each leg, 1 × 5 each leg
Hinge: 1 × 6, 1 × 5, 1 × 4
Push: 1 × 6, 1 × 5
Pull: 1 × 6, 1 × 5
Press: 1 × 6, 1 × 5
Rotation Snatch: 1 × 3 speed
Auxiliary (Calf): 1 × 20 each leg
Auxiliary (Post Delt Raise): 1 × 10
Auxiliary (Curl): 1 × 10

Week 2

Rest 40 seconds between exercises.

DAY 1

Squat: 1 × 6, 1 × 5
Lunge: 1 × 6 each leg, 1 × 5 each leg
Hinge: 1 × 6, 1 × 5
Push: 1 × 6, 1 × 5, 1 × 4
Pull: 1 × 6, 1 × 5, 1 × 4
Press: 1 × 6, 1 × 5, 1 × 4
Rotation Snatch: 1 × 3 speed
Auxiliary (Calf): 1 × 20 each leg
Auxiliary (Lateral Raise): 1 × 10
Auxiliary (Curl): 1 × 10

DAY 2

Perform with a light weight and emphasize speed of movement, keeping good technique.
Squat: 1 × 6, 1 × 5
Lunge: 1 × 6 each leg, 1 × 5 each leg
Hinge: 1 × 6, 1 × 5
Push: 1 × 6, 1 × 5, 1 × 4
Pull: 1 × 6, 1 × 5, 1 × 4
Press: 1 × 6, 1 × 5, 1 × 4
Rotation Snatch: 1 × 3 speed
Auxiliary (Calf): 1 × 20 each leg
Auxiliary (Post Delt Raise): 1 × 10
Auxiliary (Curl): 1 × 10

Week 3

Rest 35 seconds between exercises.

DAY 1

Squat: 1 × 6, 1 × 5, 1 × 4

Lunge: 1 × 6 each leg, 1 × 5 each leg

Hinge: 1 × 6, 1 × 5, 1 × 4

Push: 1 × 6, 1 × 5, 1 × 4

Pull: 1 × 6, 1 × 5, 1 × 4

Press: 1 × 6, 1 × 5, 1 × 4

Rotation Snatch: 1 × 3 speed

Auxiliary (Calf): 1 × 20 each leg

Auxiliary (Lateral Raise): 1 × 10

Auxiliary (Curl): 1 × 10

DAY 2

Perform with a light weight and emphasize speed of movement, keeping good technique.

Squat: 1 × 6, 1 × 5, 1 × 4

Lunge: 1 × 6 each leg, 1 × 5 each leg

Hinge: 1 × 6, 1 × 5, 1 × 4

Push: 1 × 6, 1 × 5, 1 × 4

Pull: 1 × 6, 1 × 5, 1 × 4

Press: 1 × 6, 1 × 5, 1 × 4

Rotation Snatch: 1 × 3 speed

Auxiliary (Calf): 1 × 20 each leg

Auxiliary (Post Delt Raise): 1 × 10

Auxiliary (Curl): 1 × 10

Week 4

Rest 30 seconds between exercises.

DAY 1:

Squat: 1 × 6, 1 × 5, 1 × 4

Lunge: 1 × 6 each leg, 1 × 5 each leg, 1 × 4 each leg

Hinge: 1 × 6, 1 × 5, 1 × 4

Push: 1 × 6, 1 × 5, 1 × 4

Pull: 1 × 6, 1 × 5, 1 × 4

Press: 1 × 6, 1 × 5, 1 × 4

Rotation Snatch: 1 × 3 speed

Auxiliary (Calf): 1 × 20 each leg

Auxiliary (Lateral Raise): 1 × 10

Auxiliary (Curl): 1 × 10

DAY 2

Perform with a light weight and emphasize speed of movement, keeping good technique.

Squat: 1 × 6, 1 × 5, 1 × 4

Lunge: 1 × 6 each leg, 1 × 5 each leg, 1 × 4 each leg

Hinge: 1 × 6, 1 × 5, 1 × 4

Push: 1 × 6, 1 × 5, 1 × 4

Pull: 1 × 6, 1 × 5, 1 × 4

Press: 1 × 6, 1 × 5, 1 × 4

Rotation Snatch: 1 × 3 speed

Auxiliary (Calf): 1 × 20 each leg

Auxiliary (Post Delt Raise): 1 × 10

Auxiliary (Curl): 1 × 10

TRANSITION: ONE TO TWO WEEKS

In this phase, you take time off so you can come back stronger and ready to start another training cycle. The recovery phase is also called a transition phase because it helps you enter the new cycle at a higher level. During this phase, you don't just lie on the couch. You stay active but at a decreased intensity, and you choose activities that involve different movement patterns.

This is the time to be curious and try something new. You might add Pilates. Or yoga. Or MovNat (or any of the primitive movement workouts). Or take a ballroom dancing class.

As for pickleball, this might be a month when you focus on drills and practice. This transition phase also provides an opportunity to work on a part of your body that needs some extra attention.

9.

THE CORE TRAINING

The concept of core is both old and new. It goes back to ancient traditions of martial arts and yoga and is at the center of modern physical practices like Pilates. Although we hear the core talked about a lot in the world of fitness and sports, we need to start with a clear definition.

Your core is not just your abs. It encompasses your entire spine and the muscles of your back, hips, and pelvic area. It's a 360-degree matrix comprised of small, deep stabilization muscles and large, powerful muscles like the gluteus maximus. As the body's hub, the core initiates movements, and movements are transferred from the ground up and from the top down. A strong core enables you to move fluidly and powerfully in all directions, keeping you stable (an immovable pillar of strength) against forces that can come from any direction. A strong core is essential for balance, agility, postural alignment, spinal support, and powerful, explosive movements.

THE FOUR-WAY CORE

For this reason, our core system has four elements. We train your core to be stable in an isometric hold (iso hold), to move with rotational power, to develop anti-rotational strength, and to have an athletic, reactive response. We also train in multiple positions: on the floor, on all fours, and on your feet.

Core training enhances your pickleball performance by providing a solid foundation for athletic movements. A strong and stable core enhances your ability to transfer power to your arms and legs for backhands and ground strokes. Your core strength also improves your balance, agility, and overall athletic ability, giving you on-court confidence and preventing hip and back injuries.

THE INNER CORE

The inner core is composed of a group of deep muscles that work together to provide stability and support to the spine and pelvis, forming the foundation of core strength and function. The inner core's main muscles are:

- *Transverse abdominis (TVA)*. This muscle is the deepest layer of the abdominal muscles and wraps around the torso like a corset. The TVA plays a crucial role in core stability by supporting the spine.

- *Multifidus*. The multifidus muscle is a series of small bundles of fibers located along the spine. It plays a vital role in maintaining proper spinal alignment and stability.

- *Diaphragm*. While commonly associated with breathing, the diaphragm also plays a role in core stability. This dome-shaped muscle separates the thoracic and abdominal cavities and aids in stabilizing the spine.

- *Pelvic floor muscles*. The pelvic floor muscles form a hammock-like structure at the base of the pelvis. They support the pelvic organs and contribute to core stability by working with the other inner core muscles.

MAJOR CORE MUSCLES

The inner core muscles work in coordination with the larger outer muscles, which include:

- *Rectus abdominis.* This long muscle runs along the front of the abdomen (often referred as the "six-pack" muscles).

- *Obliques.* The obliques, along the sides of the abdomen, enable the torso's twisting and side-to-side movements.

- *Gluteus Complex.* These large muscles attach to the femur and the upper part of the pelvis. They extend and externally rotate the hips.

- *Erector spinae.* This group of muscles runs along the back of the spine and helps maintain upright posture and extension of the spine.

THE CORE ORCHESTRA

The inner and outer core are designed to work together like a great orchestra. The smaller, deep inner muscles work in sync with the bigger outer muscles. The smaller, deeper, more sensitive muscles are anticipatory; they fire microseconds before the big muscles kick in to do the heavy lifting. A common reason for back injuries is these inner and outer muscles getting out of sync, leaving the spine unprotected.

Our program is designed to promote their synchronization. We will help you maintain core stability and support throughout various movements, keeping you injury-free and at peak performance. The first exercise in the core routine, dead bug, is a good place to initiate and work on this bracing.

CORE ROUTINE: THE 360 BAKER'S DOZEN

1. Dead Bug: 20 total reps, 10 in each position.
2. Super Person: Work up to 20 reps.
3. Iso Plank Series: Work up to 30 seconds hold in each position.
   - Side Plank: Work up to 30 seconds.
   - Down Plank: Work up to 30 seconds.
   - Up Plank: Work up to 30 seconds.

4. Bicycle: 20 total reps, 10 in each position.

5. Swimming on Belly: 20 total reps, 10 in each position.

6. Side Plank with Side Leg Raise: Work up to 10 leg raises on each side.

7. Up Plank with Foot Tap: 20 total reps, 10 in each position.

8. Down Plank with Side Foot Tap: 20 total reps, 10 in each position.

9. Down Plank with Shoulder Tap: 20 total reps, 10 in each position.

10. Bird Dog: 20 total reps, 10 in each position.

11. Plank with Rotation: Work up to 10 rotations on each side.

12. Knee to the Sky with Dumbbell: 10 reps on each side.

13. Standing Reactive Knee Raise: 30 seconds on each leg.

THE EXERCISES

🏓 DEAD BUG

STARTING POSITION

Lie on your back and extend your hands toward the ceiling. Raise your knees so they are perpendicular to your torso and your shins are parallel to the ground.

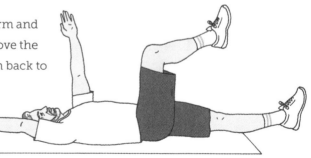

THE MOVE

On an exhale, slowly lower your right arm and your left leg until they hover just above the ground. Inhale and then bring them back to the starting position.

Repeat on the other side.

Keep your hips and low back still throughout the exercise.

Perform the movement slowly and with control.

Engage your core muscles and pelvic floor throughout the exercise.

SUPER PERSON

STARTING POSITION

Lie on your stomach on a mat.
Extend your arms over your head
and your legs straight out, your toes
touching the mat. Your head is down and your
eyes are focused on the floor.

THE MOVE

In one motion, raise your arms, torso,
and legs as if you are flying.
Hold for 3 seconds. Lower with
control to the floor, completing one
repetition.

TRAINER'S TIPS

Focus on keeping your body straight.

Align your head, neck, and spine; don't arch your back.

Focus on lengthening your body.

Initiate the movement from your body's center.

Control the lift and lowering movements.

🎾 PLANKS

STARTING POSITION 1:
DOWN PLANK

Lying on your stomach, lift your body from the floor.
Your toes and forearms or your hands bear
your weight. Your hips are lifted so the
body forms a straight plank position.

STARTING POSITION 2:
SIDE PLANK

Lying on your right side, lift your body from the floor. The outside edge of your right foot
and your right forearm or hand bear
your weight. Your hips are
lifted so the body forms
a straight plank position.
Repeat the exercise on the left side.

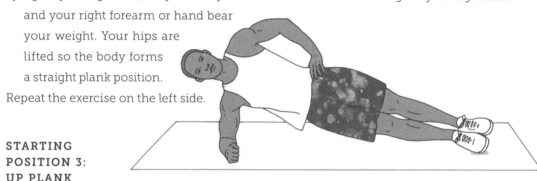

STARTING
POSITION 3:
UP PLANK

Lying on your back, lift your body from the floor. Your heels and your hands bear your
weight. Your hips are lifted so the body forms a straight plank position.

TRAINER'S TIPS

Keep your body straight as a board.
Don't allow your hips to sag.
Lengthen your neck and align it with
the spine.
Engage the core.

BICYCLES

STARTING POSITION

Lie on your back. Bring your knees over your hips, your shins parallel to the floor. Place your hands behind your head.

THE MOVE

Focus on your abs; you will move your opposite arm and leg simultaneously. One knee pulls in while the other leg straightens out at an angle.

Lift your left shoulder and rotate to your right knee; return to the starting position.

Lift your right shoulder and rotate to your left knee; return to the starting position, completing one repetition.

TRAINER'S TIPS

Feel your abs working; avoid moving too fast.

As you bicycle, be sure to twist your entire torso; don't move your elbow only.

Keep shoulder blades and legs off the floor.

Press your lower back to the floor.

 SWIMMING ON BELLY: OPPOSITE ARM AND LEG

STARTING POSITION

Lie on your stomach. Extend your arms over your head and your legs straight out. Your head is down and your eyes are focused on the floor.

THE MOVE

In one motion, raise your right arm and left leg. Hold for 3 seconds. Then lower your arm and leg to the floor.

Repeat with the opposite arm and leg, completing one repetition.

Focus on keeping your body straight.

Align your head, neck, and spine; don't arch your back.

Focus on lengthening your body.

Initiate the movement from your body's center.

Control the lift and lowering movements.

SIDE PLANK WITH SIDE LEG RAISE

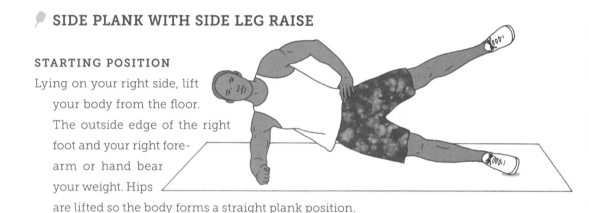

STARTING POSITION

Lying on your right side, lift your body from the floor. The outside edge of the right foot and your right forearm or hand bear your weight. Hips are lifted so the body forms a straight plank position.

THE MOVE

Raise your top leg straight up in alignment with your body. Hold for a 3 count and lower. Repeat on the other side.

UP PLANK WITH FOOT TAP

STARTING POSITION: UP PLANK

Lying on your back, lift your body from the floor. Your heels and your hands bear your weight. Hips are lifted so the body forms a straight plank position.

THE MOVE

Lift your right foot, leg straight, and hold for three seconds. Lower your leg.

Repeat on the opposite side, completing one repetition.

TRAINER'S TIPS

Focus on keeping your body in a perfect plank position.

Align your head, neck, spine, hip, knee, and ankle.

DOWN PLANK WITH SIDE FOOT TAP

STARTING POSITION:
DOWN PLANK

Assume the down plank position. Your hands or elbows
and the balls of your feet bear your
weight. Hips are lifted so the body
forms a straight plank position.

THE MOVE

Step to your right with your right foot, extending out approximately 12 inches. Tap the
ground, then return to the starting position.

Repeat with the left foot.

TRAINER'S TIPS

Focus on keeping your body in a perfect plank position as you reach out and tap with
your foot.

As you gain more strength and stability, challenge yourself by reaching your foot out
farther.

🏓 DOWN PLANK WITH SHOULDER TAP

STARTING POSITION: DOWN PLANK

Assume the down plank position. Your hands or elbows
and the balls of your feet bear your weight.
Hips are lifted so the body forms a
straight plank position.

THE MOVE

Lift your right hand and reach across your body to touch your left shoulder. Return to the
starting position.
Repeat the movement with your left hand.

TRAINER'S TIPS

Focus on keeping your body perfectly aligned, with no dropping of the hip when you
reach across your body.
Align your head, neck, spine, hip, knee, and ankle.

🏓 BIRD DOG WITH SPEED AND HOLD

STARTING POSITION

Assume a tabletop position on all fours.
Align your arms and wrists with your shoulders, and
your knees with your hips. Your head should be in line with your body, eyes down.

THE MOVE

In one motion and with speed, lift your
arm and leg until they are parallel to
the floor. Initiate the movement from your
core. Lock in and hold that position for a
3 count.
Repeat on other side.

Don't use momentum; lift with control.

Get as close to parallel as you can.

PLANK WITH ROTATION

STARTING POSITION: SIDE PLANK

Lying on your left side, lift your body from the floor
   into the side plank position. The outside edge of
   your left foot and your left hand or elbow
   bear your weight. Your arm is
   extended straight up toward
   the sky.

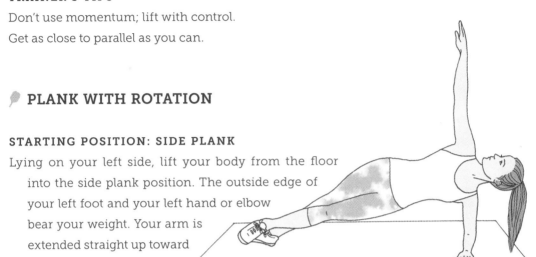

THE MOVE:

Rotate your left hip toward the floor as you thread your
   right arm under your body (between your body
   and the floor). Rotate back to the side
   plank starting position. Repeat
   for the required number of
   reps.

Switch sides and repeat the exercise.

TRAINER'S TIPS

Focus on keeping your body aligned.

Activate the rotation from the center of your body.

Focus on being long and strong.

Maintain your balance.

🏓 KNEE TO THE SKY

Body weight, dumbbell, or paddle.

STARTING POSITION

This exercise can be done with body weight, a dumbbell, or a paddle. Stand with feet shoulder width apart. Bend forward in an athletic stance with your chest up, knees bent, and your arms extended diagonally across your body at knee level.

THE MOVE

Rotate torso as you raise the weight on a diagonal to the opposite shoulder. The motion is from low to high (hip to shoulder) and to the opposite side (i.e., left knee to right shoulder). Lower and repeat.

Repeat with the same number of reps on opposite side.

TRAINER'S TIPS

Focus on keeping your back straight and your core tight. Align your head, neck, spine, hip, knee, ankle.

🏓 STANDING REACTIVE KNEE RAISE

STARTING POSITION

Stand with your feet hip width apart, your arms at your sides.

THE MOVE

Lift one knee, forming a 90-degree angle with your leg. Hold 30 seconds on each leg. Mix it up and move in all directions, playing with the edge of your balance. Here are some options: move high and low, side to side; rotate clockwise and counterclockwise with your arms extended; move diagonally (45-degree angles). Have your paddle handy and do your basic strokes with your right and left arm (dinks, ground strokes, volleys, smashes).

TRAINER'S TIPS

Engage your core muscles.

Maintain a neutral spine.

Initiate the movement from your core, not from your arms and legs.

DRILLS AND CONDITIONING

The drills in this component serve two important functions. First, they will improve your movement literacy, what we call the ABCs of movement (agility, balance, and coordination). Ultimately, the goal is to move from basic literacy toward poetry in motion on the court. Second, it will train the energy system you use for pickleball—shorter explosive bursts of energy with limited recovery time. The component improves your footwork and your ability to change directions and to accelerate and decelerate with more speed and power.

THE IMPORTANCE OF DRILLS AND MOVEMENT LITERACY FOR PICKLEBALL

The drills in this chapter, in combination with PB-150, will increase your movement vocabulary and make you a better pickleball player. They will improve:

- Your athletic posture, putting you in a ready position.
- Your spatial awareness, helping you develop a coach's eye to analyze your movement patterns.

- Your coordination, enabling you to synchronize complex sports movements.
- Your agility, enhancing your ability to change direction rapidly while accelerating and decelerating.
- Your proprioception (your sixth sense), improving your awareness of where your body is in space without relying on vision.

All these elements add up to improving your movement quality, which also decreases your risk of injury.

MOVEMENT LITERACY, PART ONE: THE ATHLETIC STANCE (THE POSITION OF READINESS)

There's a reason why pro athletes often have their feet shoulder width apart, with their knees slightly bent and their weight on the balls of their feet. This stance is the fundamental ready position. The sports world calls it the athletic stance. It provides the foundation for effective movement, balance, and stability. Your center of gravity is optimally situated between your legs, creating stability and enabling you to run, jump, and move in any direction. Sports requiring fast movements and direction changes, like pickleball, demand an athletic stance from players. When you take this stance, you can access power, speed, and agility in your movements.

HOW TO GET IN THE STANCE

Slightly bend (flex) your knees and your ankles, shifting the weight to the balls of your feet. Then move your shoulders over your knees, slightly bending at the hips. Your chest and head are upright, and your arms are at the ready, elbows bent. Notice that your ankles, knees, and hips are flexed. Sports trainers call this triple flexion. The athletic stance prepares you for powerful movements like jumping. And flexing is an effective way to load your muscles. Hence they're ready for action, prepared to explode (to complete the metaphor of "load and explode"). You can generate power, control your balance, and react quickly to changes in direction. Practicing this position consistently during workouts and on the court will improve your reaction time and explosiveness.

MOVEMENT LITERACY, PART TWO: APPLICATION OF BODY WEIGHT

An important concept for movement literacy is the application of body weight. The term sounds a little intimidating, but the concept is simple and profound. It purely means how you use your body to your advantage.

Let's look at a squat and see how it can be applied to training. First, ask yourself a few simple questions. When you perform a body-weight squat, where do you apply pressure as you rise up and with which body part? You are applying pressure or force into the ground with your feet. This key concept is called *ground force* (see the sidebar "Ground Force Pep Talk"). When you are squatting or jumping, a helpful exercise cue is to think, "Push down into the ground to rise up."

By going through this questioning process, you are pulling into your conscious mind what is happening out of its awareness, so you can analyze the effectiveness of your body movements. You are now becoming a movement nerd, in a good way.

In many exercises involving body weight, different body parts work independently (not in unison, as with a squat). A lunge is a good example. To perform a lunge with your left leg, drive off your right leg, applying force into the ground at an angle that initiates a step forward with your left leg. When the left foot makes contact with the ground, your body weight shifts primarily to that leg (your right leg still provides some ground force to support the move). Then you push off your left foot to return to the starting position.

Pushing off the ground to return to your starting position is a helpful cue when lunging.

MOVEMENT LITERACY, PART THREE: CENTER OF GRAVITY

Your center of gravity is the place where your body's weight is equally balanced in all directions. When you're standing, your center of gravity is about an inch or two below your belly button. Every time your body changes position, your center of gravity is altered, too. The center of gravity in the human body is dynamic.

One thing we all try to do each day is avoid falling. As we age, falling becomes a major fear and one of the primary reasons for medical complications and death. When we were babies, we also had to manage this learning curve, but we did so in the spirit of exploration and fun. Great movers—athletes and dancers—have mastered their awareness of their center of gravity and turned movement from a daily function (a vitally important one) into a physical expression of their art or sport. Training for pickleball offers the opportunity to return to the spirit of moving you delighted in as a baby when you were taking your first steps.

Your center of gravity is your first responder. It effectively allows you to optimize how you apply your body weight. Your center of gravity and your body weight are always working in tandem for better or for worse. To make this a productive partnership, you need to understand the kinetic chain and figure out how to leverage its power.

MOVEMENT LITERACY, PART FOUR: THE KINETIC CHAIN

You know the old spiritual "Dem Bones." It goes something like this:

Toe bone connected to the foot bone
Foot bone connected to the heel bone
Heel bone connected to the ankle bone
Ankle bone connected to the leg bone . . .

This song may not be precisely anatomically correct (although darn close), but it tells an important and bigger story. With movement, everything in our body is interconnected. Sports scientists (especially kinesiologists and biomechanists) call this connection the kinetic chain. As the song says, every bone adjoins another bone, connected by muscles, ligaments, and tendons that hold the structure together and enable it to move. And now we know that it's not just bones and muscle but also fascia, or connective tissue. There needs to be a fascia song.

The body is an interconnected system—one part can affect the others. PB-150 is designed to make this system work like a finely tuned orchestra. In a Venn diagram, all the PB-150 elements would overlap. The prehab routine tunes the individual joints and areas prone to injury. The dynamic warm-up links them in movement sequences. Strength training builds power through all the joints; core work creates a powerful hub to keep things moving from top to bottom in all directions. Your cooldown aids your recovery and extends and releases your full potential in small but important ways.

For any position and action, there is an optimal way for your kinetic chain to be organized (aligned). The takeaway from the kinetic chain is simple: a misalignment will increase inefficiencies and chances of injury. Sport takes you out of perfect alignment. Training helps you withstand these demands.

ON THE COURT

Let's explore how the application of body weight and center of gravity come together on the court. Harnessing the power of these two movement fundamentals (often not talked about) will help you in essential pickleball skills: performing ground strokes, volleys, and dinks and serving.

GROUND STROKES AND VOLLEYS

When preparing for ground strokes and volleys (forehand and backhand), you push off the ground, transferring the force through your kinetic chain (via the core) to make a winning shot. This allows you to generate power and accuracy. If your feet aren't set, if you're standing up too straight, and if you're timid in planting your feet, your ground strokes and volleys will not be as precise and powerful as they could be. All these issues can be alleviated by using your center of gravity and ground force in tandem.

GETTING YOUR FEET SET

One of the main objectives of the drills is to improve your speed, agility, balance, and coordination. Such improvements will make you more efficient at getting to the ball to set your feet (not having bouncy, happy feet).

PLAY LOW, NOT HIGH

You've probably heard the phrase *play low*. This means you need to lower your center of gravity so you can effectively apply ground force. When your center of gravity is high, you can't apply powerful ground force. Learning to sync these two will improve your game.

With ground strokes and volleys, being set and playing low allows you to make a variety of choices in how hard or soft you choose to hit the ball, depending on the game strategy.

APPLYING GROUND FORCE

Being timid with planting your feet can be overcome with practice. Applying ground force is a skill. Being loaded in your athletic stance will help you take this step.

DINKS AND SERVING

DINKS

All the elements above apply to dinks. Getting in position for dinks requires efficient footwork, as well as playing low and applying ground force. With these elements under your control, your dinking will be more accurate and you'll improve your touch.

SERVING

Serving is more a controlled stroke. Increased development of these skills allows you to calibrate your serve more accurately and consistently. If your goal is to drive your serve deep, you can do this with more consistency.

INJURIES:
UP THE CHAIN AND DOWN THE CHAIN

You twist your ankle playing pickleball. It happens. It swells a little and hurts for a few days, but soon the swelling decreases, and you feel fine. No biggie, it was just a sprained ankle. You get back on the court. But it's common to lose a little mobility in your ankle. When this happens, the ankle has a harder time doing its job effectively. So the knee has to take over to provide some lateral stability—something it is not primarily designed to do. Suddenly, you have knee pain, and you can't remember doing anything to hurt your knee. You've forgotten all about your sprained ankle, and you haven't sung the "Dem Bones" song since you were a kid.

Often an injury happens not because a traumatic event occurs but because a joint is forced to compensate for a problem above or below it. Your prehab routine is designed to help prevent this common problem by restoring full mobility and stability to the affected area. In this scenario, you most likely would have corrected this ankle mobility issue and have never had the knee problem. In this case, the prehab moves for your ankle magically turn into a rehab routine for your ankle sprain, solving your problem before it even becomes one.

Muscle imbalance, overtraining, and overusing the same movement pattern can also cause problems. This is why exercising the body in all three planes of motion is important for decreasing imbalances and improving your movement potential in all directions.

PICKLEBALL AGILITY, BALANCE, SPEED, AND CONDITIONING DRILLS

These drills are designed to improve your:

1. Speed in all directions.
2. Ability to accelerate and decelerate.
3. Agility (efficient and explosive changes of direction).

The drills address movement patterns on the pickleball court. During your first month of training, learn and practice the drills without a paddle. Once you've mastered the basic movements of the drill, perform one drill session each week with your paddle.

Guidelines for Performing the Drills

1. Master the movements and slowly add intensity. Walk and jog through the drills for the first few sessions. On the box drill, take your time between jumps. See the Max Effort Guidelines below for increasing intensity.

2. Warm up before performing the drills. As part of PB-150, these drills are preceded by a dynamic warm-up session to prepare you.

3. Rest for the recommended time between drills so you can recover adequately. Then you can perform the next drill with full effort.

4. Be precise when you perform the drill. Don't cut corners or stop short.

Max Effort Guidelines

1. Build up slowly to a more intense effort.

2. For the first two weeks, work at 50 percent max effort (5 on your RPE scale) as

your body's muscles, balance, and coordination adjust to the demands of the drills.

3. In Weeks 2 to 4, work at 70 percent max effort (7 on your RPE scale).

4. In Month 2, work at 80 to 90 percent max effort (an 8 or 9 on your RPE scale).

FOOTWORK BASICS

In pickleball, your footwork is critical for making effective shots. You'll practice these essential steps in the drills. For a discussion of the athletic stance, refer back to "Movement Literacy, Part One: The Athletic Stance" on page 116.

CROSS-STEP

The cross-step is used to cover a large piece of pickleball real estate quickly, especially moving to your side (laterally). You cross-step when a ball is hit far to one side (close to the out-of-bounds line). Instead of taking multiple side steps, cross one foot over the other, turning your entire body toward the ball.

THE MOVE

Get in your athletic stance.

Identify: The direction of the ball.

React: To move left, shift your weight to your left leg as you cross your right leg in front of your left leg, squaring your shoulders and sprinting to the ball.

Decelerate: To a place of stability to hit your shot.

SPLIT STEP

The split step preps your body to react quickly to your opponent's shot. It loads your body to move with power, like compressing a spring. You can think "load and explode" (we know this sounds a little violent). The split step is a small hop just as your opponent is about to hit the ball, which leaves you in a balanced position with your ankle, knee, and hip joints slightly bent, ready to spring into action.

THE MOVE

Get in your athletic stance.

Identify: The moment when your opponent has just made contact with the ball, and initiate your small hop, loading your body.

React: Move in the direction of the incoming ball.

Decelerate: To a place of stability, hit your shot, and reposition in your athletic stance.

🏓 LATERAL (SIDE) STEP

The lateral or side step is a fundamental footwork move to cover short, lateral distances on the court. You move sideways while staying balanced and prepared to hit your next shot.

THE MOVE

Get in your athletic stance.

Identify: The direction you need to move, left or right. Watch the ball as your opponent hits it, improving your anticipation.

React: To move right, push off with your left foot and step laterally to the right. To move left, push off your right foot and step laterally. Repeat this motion to cover more territory. This initial push will give you the momentum needed to cover the ground quickly.

Decelerate: To a place of stability to hit your shot and reposition in your athletic stance.

THE DRILLS

🏓 STAR DRILL

The starting point is the center of the star; imagine lines moving from it in all directions. Each line extends out 20 feet. If you don't have this amount of space, extend lines out as far you can while keeping it safe.

Face the same direction for all movements, as if you're looking at the net on a pickleball court.

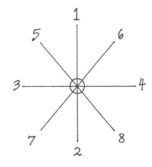

Each line – 20 ft

Start in a good athletic position.

For each movement, run the length of the line.

If you're on an unmarked floor, place an object (such as a pickleball) at the end point of an imaginary line. You will move toward that object, seeing the line in your mind's eye. See our diagram for a visual.

THE DIRECTIONS

Sprint forward and then backpedal to return to the center position.

Sprint forward on the left diagonal line. Backpedal to return to center.

Sprint forward on the right diagonal line. Backpedal to return to center.

Lateral shuffle to the left, then shuffle to return to center. Shuffle to the right, then shuffle to return to center.

Backpedal straight back. Sprint forward to center.

Backpedal diagonal left. Sprint forward to center.

Backpedal diagonal right. Sprint forward to center.

TRAINER'S TIPS

Work up slowly to a safe maximum speed.

Keep your head looking forward.

When you reach the point of direction change, drop your hips to absorb the load and improve your position to accelerate in the opposite direction.

VARIATIONS

Cross-step on the left and right lateral runs. After you cross-step, turn and run toward the sideline.

Perform a split step before each change of direction.

Hops: Instead of running to each direction, take one hop (both feet) in all eight directions and then hop back to the center spot. The hop should be at least one foot in each direction. Do one set moving clockwise and one counterclockwise.

Overhead jumps: While running to each spot, perform a vertical jump, mimicking an overhead slam with your paddle arm. Then return to the starting position.

T-DRILL SPRINT AND LATERAL SHUFFLE

THE DIRECTIONS

Start at the center line/baseline in a good athletic position.

Sprint to the kitchen line, decelerate, and then shuffle with a lateral step to the right sideline. Still facing the net, turn and jog in a quarter circle to the starting position.

Sprint to the kitchen line, stop, and shuffle with a lateral step to the left sideline. Still facing the net, turn and jog in a quarter circle to the starting position.

TRAINER'S TIPS

Perform at a safe maximum speed, except jog slowly on the quarter circle back to the starting position.

Keep your head looking forward.

When you reach the kitchen, drop your butt to absorb the load of deceleration and improve your position to accelerate toward the left or right sideline.

Don't cross your feet when performing the left and right lateral movements.

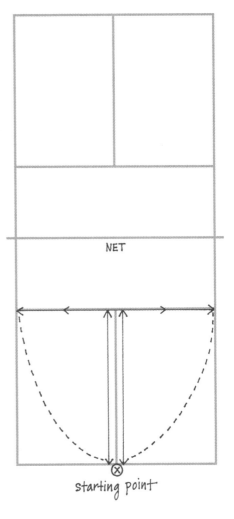

NET

starting point

SPRINT AND CROSSOVER

Start at the center line/baseline in a good athletic position.

Sprint to the kitchen, stop, cross-step to the right, and run to the right sideline.

Circle back to the starting position, keeping the proper shoulder and head position angled toward the net.

Repeat, crossing over to the left, running to the left sideline, and circling back.

🏓 HALF CIRCLE

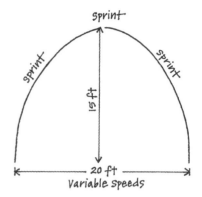

Start at the base center line in a good athletic position.

Shuffle with a lateral step to the left sideline. Still facing the net, then sprint a quarter circle to the kitchen line.

Back pedal to the center baseline, then shuffle with lateral steps to the right sideline. At the sideline sprint the quarter circle, curving back to the baseline on the left side, then back pedal to the center of the court.

TRAINER'S TIPS

Perform the drill at a safe maximum speed.

Keep your head facing forward.

When you reach the sideline, drop your butt to absorb the load. Open your hips to the inside so you are in position to sprint in the quarter circle while keeping your head and shoulders turned toward the net.

VARIATIONS

Turn and run to the sideline rather than slide.

🏓 FOUR SQUARE HOPS

In this drill, you will hop to designated boxes a required number of times, with either one foot or two feet.

Begin performing each variation with both feet. As you progress, incorporate more one-foot movements.

For one-foot patterns, do an equal number with both the left foot and the right.

BASIC TWO-FEET AND ONE-FOOT PATTERNS

Each box is numbered: 1, 2, 3, 4.

Side/side (from box 1 to 2): 10 reps.

Forward/back (from box 1 to 3): 10 reps.

Angle (from box 1 to 4) and (from box 3 to 2): 10 reps.

Around the world (from box 1 to 2 to 4 to 1), then reverse (1, 3, 4, 1) to complete one round. Do three rounds.

TRAINER'S TIPS

Perform the drill at safe maximum speed.

Keep your knees bent, with your butt down.

Maintain a good athletic posture with the upper body.

Practice the patterns slowly a few times so that you learn the pattern before progressing to full speed.

VARIATIONS

Three-box patterns: for example, 1 to 2 to 4. Repeat for the number of touches or time. If possible, perform both the pattern and its opposite. For example, the opposite of 1 to 2 to 4 would be 2 to 1 to 3.

SPEED VARIATIONS

In this drill, you run forward, sideways, and backward. The emphasis is on changing gears when moving in these patterns and directions. Incorporate slow, medium, and fast speeds in each direction that you move. You are running a box in a counterclockwise direction. Repeat the drill in a clockwise direction.

Start at the right corner baseline in a good athletic position. You will face the net throughout this drill.

Following the sideline, run forward to the opposite baseline corner, shifting your speed from slow to medium to fast (your three gears).

Turning toward the net, shuffle with lateral steps along the baseline to the opposite corner, shifting your speed from slow to medium to fast.

At the other baseline corner, immediately run backward the length of the court to the opposite corner, shifting your speed from slow to medium to fast.

At the corner, shuffle with lateral steps to the right baseline corner where you started, shifting your speed from slow to medium to fast.

TRAINER'S TIPS

Make your speed changes fluidly, like a car changing gears.

As you get comfortable with the drill, make your change of direction faster.

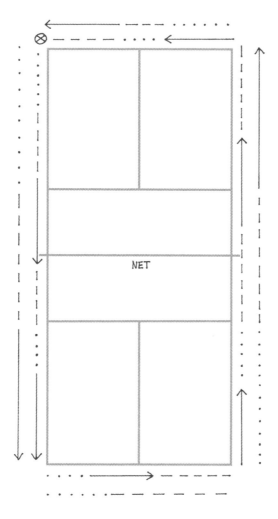

KEY:
⊗ Start
. . . . Slow
– – – – Medium
———→ Fast
Outside loop: Warm-up
Inside loop: Variable speeds

11.

COOLDOWN

A cooldown is designed to return your body, both physically and mentally, to its pre-workout state and to begin the recovery process. The PB-150 cooldown consists of two simple techniques: gentle stretching and a transformative breath pattern. Our program contains ten stretches and the 6-Breaths-in-a-Minute Method.

STATIC STRETCHING

Experts have questioned whether static stretching is a wise use of time for people who are already doing a dynamic warm-up and an array of multi-joint strength training movements. Yet respected organizations like the American College of Sports Medicine still consider static stretching to be an important component in a cooldown program. Without going too deeply into the debates, we'll reframe the benefits of static stretching at the end of a workout and integrate it with breathing.

RELEASE AND RESTORE STRETCHING

Instead of calling it simply stretching or flexibility work, let's refer to this process as release and restore stretching (RRS), a new kind of R & R. After a vigorous workout or pickleball match, the muscles can be contracted and tight. Additionally, aspects of everyday living such as sitting too much or carrying heavy groceries can make your muscles stiff with partial contractions. But what does this mean?

Simply put, the theory of sliding myofilaments describes how muscles work. Your muscles are made up of a series of overlapping fibers. When you contract the muscle, these fibers slide together and shorten, causing joint flexion. Think of a biceps curl. When the biceps muscle contracts, your hand moves toward the shoulder. The opposite happens when the arm extends and straightens. The muscle fibers slide apart. When you stretch, the fibers slide even farther apart. When the muscle fibers reach their limit, tension is transferred to the tendons, which become more pliable.

Stretching sets off a little alarm in the body, creating a contraction to stop the muscle from lengthening. This reflex is designed to prevent overextension and potential injury. Sudden explosive movements trigger a more powerful contraction to inhibit the movement. But if you move slowly and gently, your muscles gradually release and lengthen. When you patiently hold and breathe, the alarm signals subside and the body calms down and releases.

This process can help you extend your end range of motion in a movement or joint. As a result, you will have a greater range of motion in your strength training and dynamic warm-up. This in turn means you have more strength and stability throughout your increased range of motion. So during a pickleball game, when you passionately lunge and reach to return a ball, you'll be more powerful and injury-resistant through that extended range. Let's call that your competition range of motion.

By going through this routine when your body is warm, you accomplish some important things at a functional level: you release and restore the muscle to a pliable pre-workout state, and in a gentle, patient way, you extend the end range of the movement.

But the benefits go beyond this. Recent research presents a paradigm shift from the traditional exercise physiological view of stretching as measuring range of motion. In fact, the deeper importance of stretching ultimately may not be about its contribution to flexibility. Rather, stretching may change our body all the way down to our cells, decreasing inflammation.

In a 2016 study, Dr. Helene Langevin, the director of the National Center for Complementary and Integrative Health (NCCIH), along with a team at Harvard University injected rats with carrageenan to promote inflammation. Then they encouraged half of the rats to stretch in a position similar to downward dog. They found that "using rodent models has begun to suggest a link between stretching and the resolution of inflammation within connective tissue." Areas of inflammation were significantly reduced in the rats that stretched, and their tissues contained fewer white blood cells.

This makes the benefits of stretching go beyond feats of flexibility, since inflammation is implicated in many serious diseases, including Alzheimer's, Parkinson's, heart disease, and cancer. Future research looks to shed more light on this.

THE 6-BREATHS-IN-A-MINUTE METHOD

In this routine, you'll integrate a specific breathing pattern. Research has developed a doable method to manage your breath for an array of physical, mental, and emotional health benefits. With the 6-Breaths-in-a-Minute Method, you will inhale for a 5 count and exhale for a 5 count, both through the nose.

The discovery of this magic number was originally made by a team in Italy. The Italian team wired participants for basic physiological and neurological feedback and had them recite Buddhist mantras, rosaries in Latin, and the Catholic Ava Maria, or Hail Mary (it was Italy, after all). They were astonished that all these religious texts had the same breath cycle, six breaths per minute. This breathing pattern enabled basic body functions to work at peak efficiency.

Two American researchers, Dr. Richard Brown and Dr. Patricia Gerbarg, built on the research and repeated the experiment, minus the religious element. They worked with patients suffering from depression and anxiety. These patients ultimately found peace at the same rhythm, basically six breaths per minute. They felt relief after doing this practice for as little as five minutes. The cycle leads to an inner sense of calmness. The rhythm seems to be naturally soothing. Your cooldown routine will combine this breathing pattern with stretching to gently release and restore. The power of breathwork is starting to hit the mainstream fitness culture, thanks to user-friendly books by Brown and Gerbarg and James Nestor's book, *Breath: The New Science of a Lost Art.*

COOLDOWN ROUTINE

Here is your cooldown routine, partially inspired by rats doing downward dogs, religious prayers, secular-scientific interventions helping those suffering from depression and anxiety, and anecdotal feedback from fitness and movement practitioners. The cooldown also brings us full circle. The book's goal is holistic—to engage your brain, body, and spirit.

THE ROUTINE

- Complete the series of eight moves below and hold each stretch for 30 seconds.
- As you go through the routine, breathe in a rhythm of 6 breaths per minute.
- Think about release and restore stretching (RRS) with each position, gently performing the stretch so your body gradually releases.
- In each position, think of how you are organizing your body in the proper form. Feel the form of the stretch from the inside out.

THE POSITIONS

When stretching, always execute the stretch until you feel a release of tightness, not pain. Overstretching can be harmful and isn't conducive to the desired effect. Hold each stretch for 30 seconds. Create a sense of flow as you move between exercises.

🏓 KNEES TO CHEST

Lying on your back, pull both knees into your chest, wrapping both arms around your knees or your shins. Tuck your chin, if this feels comfortable. If not, let your head rest on the ground. Hold for 30 seconds. Release your legs and straighten them. Remain on your back and perform the leg over stretch.

HAMSTRING STRETCH

Lie on your back with your legs straight. Bring your right knee toward your chest, then straighten the leg. Grasp the back of the leg with both hands and gently pull your leg forward until you feel a mild stretch. Keep your left leg straight and on the floor during the stretch. Hold for 30 seconds. Repeat with the left leg.

SEATED FORWARD BEND

Sitting with legs straight in front of you, inhale and reach with both hands toward the ceiling, shifting your weight up and onto your sitting bones. Then exhale, reaching forward with your hands toward your toes. Give into gravity as you reach and release into the stretch. Reach only to a point of tightness, not of pain. Hold for 30 seconds and return to where you started. Spread both legs into a V-formation and keep straight to perform the V-Stretch.

V-STRETCH

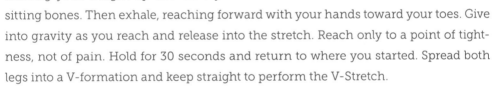

Sit up straight, high on your sitting bones, with legs spread in the shape of a V. Turn your torso toward your right leg and reach toward your right toes. Reach only to a point of tightness, not of pain. Hold for 30 seconds and return to the starting position. Turn your torso toward your left leg and perform the same stretch on your left side. Hold for 30 seconds and return to the starting position. Change positions so that you are face down on your stomach with legs extended straight behind you and slightly apart. Perform the cobra.

🏓 COBRA

Place your hands next to your shoulders in a push-up position. Keeping your hips and legs down on the ground, push up your upper torso by straightening your arms. Push up to tightness, not pain. Ideally, you will straighten your arms completely, but that may not be possible initially, so stop and hold when you feel tightness or when your hips start to leave the ground. Hold for 30 seconds, then come up to your hands and knees to perform the cat-cow.

🏓 CAT-COW

Get on all fours in neutral spine (also known as the tabletop position). Your hands should be directly under your shoulders and your knees should be under your hips. The tops of your feet should be flat on the mat. Round your back up toward the ceiling like an angry cat; your back should feel tight. Tuck your chin to your chest and let your head drop down. Then tuck your tailbone and press down through your hands to open your back. Hold for 5 seconds. Return to the starting position.

Drop your belly down toward the floor, lifting your head and tailbone toward the ceiling. Look straight ahead or slightly upward, whichever feels most comfortable for your neck. This is the cow position. Hold for 5 seconds.

Repeat rounding your back and arching it downward with 5-second holds two more times. This will result in 3 repetitions of each position (rounded up and arched down).

CHILD'S POSE

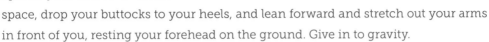

Stay on your hands and knees, keeping the tops of your feet on the floor. Spread your knees to create space, drop your buttocks to your heels, and lean forward and stretch out your arms in front of you, resting your forehead on the ground. Give in to gravity.

When finished, bring your right knee up and forward to a lunge position with your right foot flat on the floor and your left knee remaining on the ground to transition into a hip flexor stretch.

HIP FLEXOR STRETCH

With your left knee forward in a kneeling lunge position and your left foot flat on the floor, while your right knee remains on the ground, place both hands on your left knee and lean forward so that your right hip and quad feel the stretch. Lean forward to tightness and hold for 30 seconds. Return to both knees and then bring the right knee forward to the lunge position while your left knee remains on the ground. Repeat the stretch for 30 seconds on this side.

FOAM ROLLING

TO ROLL OR NOT TO ROLL? ROLL! THE PROS DO IT

Many people have foam rollers that end up living in their closets or leaning in a basement corner, gathering dust. Then there are others who are on and off their foam roller all day and who consistently preach the benefits with a religious zeal. For pro teams and elite private training facilities, foam rolling is a mandatory part of a complete training program. As is true with any fitness practice, you have to foam roll consistently to see sustained results. The simplest and perhaps most motivating way to think about foam rolling is that it's like giving yourself a sports massage.

Here is the key to foam rolling success: you have to develop a relationship with your foam roller in order for the habit to stick. This takes a little time (give it at least three weeks). In the context of fitness, this relationship is actually kind of intimate. You and your foam roller have to get to know each other, spend some quality time together, and get in a flow. Communication is key. Together you will discover your sensitive spots and tight areas. Everyone is different. For some, the hip flexors and psoas muscle are tight, and for others, the upper back may be a trouble spot. The foam roller begins to know you as you say with feeling, "Ahhh, yes, right there, that's the spot." Once that relationship has evolved, you, too, are likely to become one of those converts.

After our initial guidance, you may discover little tweaks and improvisations around the fundamentals, like a jazz player going on a riff. Listening to a little jazz while foam rolling is not a bad combo. Throughout the day, you may find yourself indulging in little micro sessions for a quick release of a problem area. You may keep a foam roller in the trunk of your car and travel with it on planes.

From our holistic point of view of the complete training model for the pickleball player, foam rolling fulfills an important part of your program, the soft tissue work or myofascial work. Let's take a little dive into what foam rolling does and why it is important. We'll do this by looking at the fascial system—a network of connective tissue found below the skin—and the role it plays in wellness and pickleball performance. As Thomas Myers, one of the inspiring leaders in investigating and explaining the importance of working the fascia, says, "Fascia is the Cinderella of body tissues, anatomically misunderstood and systematically ignored." Let's start by giving the fascia a shout-out.

FASCIA: THE BENEFITS OF BUILDING A HEALTHY FASCIAL NETWORK

To excite you about the power of a healthy fascial system, we will first outline its benefits, then get into a more detailed look at this network. Below are four big benefits for your pickleball game specifically.

Movement Efficiency: A healthy fascial network connects different muscles and muscle groups, allowing them to work together in a coordinated manner. This coordination ensures that movement is efficient and synchronized.

Mobility and Stability: A healthy fascial network provides both the structural support and the stability needed to maintain proper alignment, balance, and coordination during exercise and playing sports. The fascial network also signals for and allows joint mobility and range of motion during movement.

Power Generation: A healthy fascial system acts as a springlike mechanism, storing and releasing elastic energy. It enhances your body's ability to generate force by assisting in the transfer of forces between muscles while optimizing your speed, power, and agility. The interconnectedness of fascia allows these forces to be distributed and shared across multiple muscle groups, joints, and regions.

Communication: Healthy fascia not only connects structures within localized regions but also establishes connections over long distances in the body. For example, fascial lines can link the feet to the head or connect the back to the front of the body. This global connectivity allows for coordinated movements. It facilitates the transfer of forces across different body segments. Fascia contains various sensory receptors that provide feedback and information about body position, movement, and tension. The receptors increase proprioception and body awareness while enabling precise and coordinated movement.

A FASCIA PRIMER: SO WHAT DOES THIS SUPERSTRUCTURE ACTUALLY LOOK LIKE?

With breakthroughs in imaging technology, a clearer vision of the role of fascia is emerging, and its powerful and pervasive influence is becoming clear. In brief, your fascia is layers of connective tissue. The tissues form spiderlike webs that crisscross and weave through your body, connecting and holding in place muscles, bones, and organs. Fascia can be categorized into three main types:

- A superficial layer located just below the skin.
- A deep, more dense, fibrous layer that surrounds muscles, bones, and joints.
- Visceral fascia, which surrounds and supports the internal organs.

These three layers communicate with one another and work together.

Think of this system as a fascial network. Like a cellular fiber network that connects your phone, computer, and television, fascial fibers communicate through all the levels and functions of your body. This pervasive and integrated network is vital to your wellness and optimal physical performance. As part of the complete program, a method for tuning up this network is essential for wellness, performance, and daily pain-free function.

When healthy, this network assists the body function optimally. But like any network, it requires regular maintenance. Daily life takes its toll on our fascial system. Inactivity, such as sitting for long periods at your work computer, can cause the fascial system to become stiff and gummy. Your fascia can develop adhesions or knots, along with global muscle tightness or localized knots of tension. Likewise, if a muscle is overused or the body does a lot of repetitive motions, adhesions or knots can result, leaving the fascia in need of a little love. The good news is foam rolling will increase your range of motion without having a negative effect on your body's ability to generate force.

ENTER FOAM ROLLING

Foam rolling can keep your fascial system responsive and running smoothly, helping your muscles and movements stay in a fluid conversation. Restrictions within the fascia can lead to muscular tension, pain, and potential injury. But because your fascia is in conversation with the rest of your body as well, problematic muscles and joints can also negatively impact fascia. Muscle imbalances and joints with a limited range of motion can also affect your fascial network. That's why we address both through our prehab routine, our dynamic warm-up, and a balanced strength program. Healthy fascia also depend on hydration and stress management, which is why we have chapters on nutrition and sports psychology.

HOW TO FOAM ROLL

Here is a rundown of the basic technique.

Roll each area at a slow pace and breathe into the area you're targeting.

Avoid using excessive force, which can cause discomfort or even injury. On a scale of 1 to 10, 1 being the least amount of force and 10 being the maximum, roll out at a level 3. The goal is patience and consistency. Take the time to get used to the moves and how they feel.

If you roll on a knot or rough spot, work the area above and below to help release it. Approach the edges of the spot from a variety of angles, like you're loosening the edges of a pancake before you flip it.

Roll through the entire length of the muscle. Roll from the origin to the insertion point of the muscle (the length of the muscle). This helps in addressing any adhesions or tightness along the entire muscle. For example, for the calf, roll from the heel up to the bottom of your knee.

Maintain proper form. As you roll, maintain good posture and alignment. Avoid overarching or slumping your back, keep your head in line with your spine, and engage your core muscles to stabilize your body. Foam rolling is a mindful whole-body activity even though you're focusing on specific areas.

Relax and continue to breathe into the area you're working. If you encounter a particularly tight or sensitive spot, pause and allow the roller's pressure to gradually alleviate the tension.

Use your body weight to control the intensity of the roll. The more body weight you place on the area, the greater the intensity.

You may support your body on your hands, feet, knees, or elbows. But you are also pressing your weight into the muscle to roll it out. Weight distribution will be intuitive; lean into what feels right for you.

Consistency is key. Foam rolling is most effective when done regularly. In PB-150, to keep your workouts to a reasonable time frame, we introduce foam rolling as a recovery day tool, knowing you want to be out on the courts. We hope, however, that this is a tool you start to use before and/or after playing, meaning you'd be rolling 3 to 5 times a week.

Listen to your body. Pay attention to how your body feels during and after foam rolling. Some discomfort or tenderness is normal, especially if you're targeting tight areas. However, if you feel sharp or intense pain, stop immediately and consult a healthcare professional.

THE EXERCISES

Think of your foam rolling routines like a yoga sequence, finding flow as you stay focused and move from body area to body area.

🦶 FOOT

From a standing position, place your right heel on the foam roller. If needed, you may hold on to something for support or do the exercise from a seated position.

Curl your toes as you roll the foam roller toward your toes. Extend your toes out and up as you roll the foam roller back toward your heel.

If standing, keep most of your weight on your standing leg.

Repeat on the left foot.

Do 3 to 5 reps on each side.

🦵 CALVES

Sit on the floor with your legs extended. Place the foam roller under your left calf. Place your hands on the floor behind you for support and to initiate and navigate the rolling.

Roll your left calf up and down from your heel to the underside of your knee.

You can place your free leg on top of the other leg for added pressure, or your foot on the floor with a bent knee.

Repeat on the right calf.

Do 3 to 5 reps on each side.

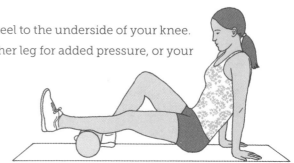

🌿 HAMSTRINGS

Sit on the floor with your left leg extended and your right leg bent with
your right foot on the floor. Place your hands on the floor
behind you for support and to initiate and
navigate the rolling.
Place the foam roller under your left ham-
string/behind the knee.
Foam roll from behind your knee to the bottom of your butt.
Repeat on the right side.
Do 3 to 5 reps on each side.

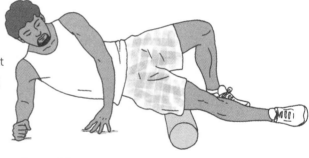

🌿 IT BAND (THE OUTSIDE OF YOUR THIGH)

Begin by lying on your right side with the foam roller positioned underneath your
thigh just above your knee. Rest
your body weight on your right
forearm. Your right leg should be
straight, and your left should be bent
at the knee with your foot placed
comfortably behind your right leg.
Use your upper body and left leg to
slowly initiate and navigate foam
rolling from your knee to the bottom of your hip.
Repeat on the left side.
Do 3 to 5 reps on each side.

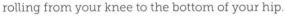

🌿 HIP FLEXOR

Start by lying face down on the floor
with the foam roller horizontal underneath your right hip.
Your left leg is bent to the side at
a comfortable angle. Rest on your right forearm.

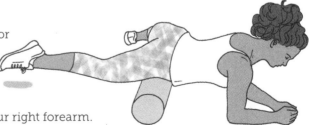

Begin to foam roll slowly up and down, targeting the hip flexor area.

Repeat with the foam roller underneath your left hip.

Do 3 to 5 reps on each side.

INNER THIGH

Lie face down on the floor, your right leg
   at an angle perpendicular to your body.
   Place the foam roller vertically on your right inner thigh just above your knee. Rest on
   both elbows for support.

Foam roll side to side from your knee to your groin area.

Repeat with the foam roller underneath your left leg.

Do 3 to 5 reps on each side.

PIRIFORMIS/GLUTES

Sit on top of the foam roller, knees bent, feet
   on the floor. Place your right ankle on
   your left knee. Angle your body to your
   right side until the foam roller is positioned on the side of your glute.

Foam roll from the bottom of your glute
   (the gluteal fold) to the top of your glute (just below your hip).

Repeat with the body angled to your left side.

Do 3 to 5 reps on each side.

UPPER BACK

Lie on the floor with the foam roller placed horizontally at your mid-back, just below your
   shoulder blades. Bend your knees so your
   feet are flat on the floor.

Place your arms behind your head and foam
   roll from below your shoulder blades to
   just below your neck.

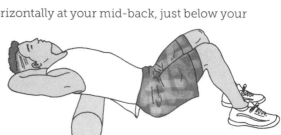

Also, play with both hugging yourself and opening up your arms out wide to your sides. Do 3 to 5 reps.

🥄 RIBS AND SHOULDERS

Lie on your right side and place the foam roller under your armpit and horizontal to your body. Keep your right leg straight and bend your left leg so your foot is on the floor behind you. Your two points of support are your left leg and your right forearm.

Slowly start to foam roll from your right armpit down the length of your rib cage.

Repeat on your left side.

Do 3 to 5 reps on each side.

PART 4

The Pickleball Wellness Lifestyle

13.

INTRODUCING PICKLEBALL WELLNESS

THE DIMENSIONS OF WELLNESS

The birth of modern wellness can be traced to Halbert L. Dunn. In 1959, in the *American Journal of Public Health*, Dunn took the word *well-being* and added fitness to it, creating a new term—*wellness*. He demonstrated the deep connection between wellness and fitness. Dunn expanded his concept in his 1961 book, *High-Level Wellness*.

Wellness involves making decisions and taking action to live a balanced life and achieve your full potential. Below you'll find the six standard dimensions of wellness—all are interrelated and affect one other.

We focus on the dimensions of physical wellness, specifically pickleball athletic physical wellness. This is more comprehensive than physical wellness for the general population. It includes developing:

- Muscular strength and power.
- Aerobic efficiency.
- Increased flexibility and range of motion in the joints.
- Agility, balance, coordination, and hand and eye coordination.
- Healthy eating habits and body composition.

- A resilient mindset.
- Injury-prevention routines.
- Self-care routines: sleep, hygiene, prevention lifestyle choices.

THE STANDARD DIMENSIONS OF WELLNESS

Physical: Integrating physical activity, exercise, healthy eating, and sleep.

Social: Maintaining and nurturing positive relationships with friends and family and romantic relationships; engaging with and contributing to one's community.

Emotional and Mental Wellness: Nurturing a positive and healthy mindset and emotional resilience; coping with stress and existential challenges.

Work: Developing a positive and meaningful connection to one's work life; achieving a healthy work-life balance.

Intellectual: Engaging in lifelong learning, critical thinking, and stimulating mental activities; cultivating your creative abilities; expanding your knowledge; and learning new skills throughout your life span.

Spiritual: Exploring and expanding a sense of harmony and meaning in life, including morals and ethics. This may or may not involve religious activities.

These components are essential for maintaining a healthy, balanced lifestyle and a meaningful life for yourself, your family, and your community. Your wellness choices also impact the wider world and the environment. Wellness is a dynamic and ongoing exploration that requires conscious effort. Each dimension contributes to overall wellness.

PICKLEBALL WELLNESS

A theme of this book has been what's good for pickleball is good for life. Pickleball is a portal into the good life: whatever you do to get better at pickleball will also make your life better. Your pickleball wellness program is designed to make you strong, energetic, and injury-resistant. What better way to move through your days? Even better, your pickleball wellness brings benefits that go beyond the physical.

Take the social dimension. The game builds friendships and community. At pickleball courts and clubs nationwide, players gather for potlucks, pizza parties, and pickleball happy hours. Venues like Chicken N Pickle bring together pickleball and socializing. *Forbes* and *The Desert Sun* both report that pickleball has become a productive way to network and make business connections.

Your pickleball wellness includes your intellectual life. The brain is stimulated whenever you learn something new, whether it be a language, a musical instrument, or pickleball. Pickleball involves learning—rules, techniques, and strategies. Because it's embodied learning, it's extra good for the brain.

For the emotional dimension of wellness, pickleball taps into passion. Sports and emotions go hand in hand. Pickleball opens up emotional expressions of joy, frustration, and anger. It helps you get in touch with and better understand your emotional makeup— the good, the bad, and the ugly. Pickleball allows you to release emotion and not repress it. Get on the court and leap into your PB-150 program with enthusiasm.

Now, you may be skeptical about pickleball's spiritual dimension—or you're nodding in agreement. Pickleball can expand one's sense of purpose and meaning in life by offering the opportunity to experience flow, self-actualization, and peak experiences. These events are often associated with spiritual growth. So are the values and ethics that sport requires us to apply. Pickleball builds character and moral excellence as we make honest calls, treat our partner with respect, and prioritize fair play. Clearly, sport is a celebration of the human spirit that carries over to everyday life.

Most important, pickleball develops our sense of play. Dr. Stuart Brown, a psychiatrist and the founder of the National Institute for Play, researches the benefits of play for human development and well-being. In his book *Play: How It Shapes the Brain, Opens the Imagination, and Invigorates the Soul*, Brown explores the scientific evidence and case studies demonstrating how play is crucial for healthy brain development, creativity, and emotional resilience. The act of playing:

- Relieves stress.
- Enhances brain function.
- Stimulates the mind and boosts creativity.
- Maintains physical fitness, strength, and flexibility.
- Improves relationships and connections with others.
- Increases productivity.
- Develops social skills.

NOURISH

Your body is capable of remarkable feats—chasing a pickleball around the court, hitting a powerful ground stroke off a bounce, or taking the ball out of the air with precision and accuracy. To honor this, you need to eat like an athlete. How you nourish yourself will significantly determine your mood, energy level, and performance on and off the court.

Jaclyn Sklaver, a licensed performance nutritionist and the founder of Athleats Nutrition, will be your performance nutritionist. Sklaver has over a decade of experience working in the trenches with pro athletes and helping people young and old eat healthy for improved performance. Moreover, Sklaver is an athlete herself. Sklaver was one of the first nutritionists to look at the demands of pickleball. Using science-based information, Sklaver will coach you through the maze of nutrition, guiding you to make intentional and healthy choices concerning foods, liquids, and supplements.

> **Sklaver:** *I always tell people, you need to treat your nutrition like you do your training and playing—with the same type of energy, commitment, planning, and seriousness. We'll focus on foundational, healthy eating principles. Nutrition for the pickleball player is more complicated than for a nonathlete. The game puts extra stresses on the body for hydration, recovery, joint health,*

and energy demands. Nutrition directly affects performance. As is true with your training, you need a foundation, an application of the basic principles to help you improve your health and performance.

MACRONUTRIENT PRIMER

ENERGIZE AND SATIATE: CARBOHYDRATES (CARBS)

There are two type of carbohydrates—simple and complex. Simple carbs, fruit and sugar, are absorbed and digested faster and are ideal to eat close to a workout, during training, and directly after a workout when we want to fuel our bodies quickly. They can be converted to energy efficiently and help with our performance as well as speed up our recovery. Complex carbohydrates are digested more slowly and release glucose into the bloodstream gradually. These are your starches, pastas, potatoes, and grains. They are great for meals where you want sustained energy and to feel full for longer periods of time. Fiber is also a form of carbohydrate, found mostly in vegetables, legumes, and fruit. Fiber helps maintain bowel health, control blood sugar, and balance cholesterol levels, among other benefits. Simple carbs such as fruit or fruit juice are digested faster than complex carbs. Each serves a different purpose when applied to performance. If you need a quick pick-me-up during prolonged exercise, you want to choose a fast-digesting simple carbohydrate. When you want sustained energy that's released more slowly, you will choose a complex carbohydrate.

Complex Carbs
Whole grains, quinoa, rice (brown, black, jasmine, basmati), oats, lentils, beans, cauliflower, lentils, chickpea pasta, edamame.

Simple Carbs
Fiber-rich fruits (apples, bananas, raspberries, blackberries, blueberries, pears, peaches, pineapple). These are also high in antioxidants.
Fiber-rich vegetables. Try avocado, broccoli, dark leafy greens, carrots, sweet potatoes with skin, artichokes, and beans.
Simple carbs to limit or avoid:

- Refined sugar and artificial/chemical sweeteners.
- Corn syrup and high-fructose corn syrup.

- Glucose, added fructose, and sucrose.
- Fruit juice concentrate.

REBUILD: PROTEIN

Lean meats, wild fish, pasture-raised eggs, tofu, milk, Greek yogurt, tempeh, edamame.

PROTECT: HEALTHY FATS

Healthy fats are important for cellular repair, cognitive abilities, regulating blood sugar, and hormones. Avocados and their oil, olives and their oil, butter from grass-fed cows, seeds (hemp, pumpkin, flax, chia), fish and fish oil, nuts and their butters.

ATHLEATS PHILOSOPHY

We may feel like our food choices are dictated by some diet trend that has hijacked our minds, including diets that exclude a group of macronutrients, which these days can be anything from fear of carbs and eating only animal protein, to eliminating seeds or oils. Sometimes we know better and do worse. We all need nourishment and hydration, and yet we're all different—influenced by our ethnic background, genetic and medical needs, family culture (what we ate growing up), and aspirational eating goals.

We do this basic life action—eating—in an ever-changing terrain of fad diets and food pyramids. We struggle to make the best decisions as we are bombarded by choices and promises. No wonder food expert Michael Pollan has flagged the basic question "What's for dinner?" as a cause of anxiety.

Other such questions have joined the list: How much water should I drink? What kind of water? What supplements should I take? How much should I eat? The list goes on and on.

Sklaver: *To avoid these trends and have an anchor so your food choices aren't controlled by emotion or convenience, you need to develop a basic philosophy. We know eating is good for the body, but it is also essential for the brain. Nutrition plays a significant role in brain function and cognitive performance. Eating a balanced diet that includes complete protein sources, fruits, vegetables, whole grains, and healthy fats supports mental clarity, focus, and concentration during matches. Don't forget your brain is fueled by carbohydrates, so a diet that is insufficient in carbs affects not only your physical performance but also your mental performance.*

At Athleats Nutrition we help establish some general principles. Our basic eating philosophy is to eat whole foods, eat organic and local, eat full meals and limit snacking, eat macronutrients in reasonable proportions, supplement with intelligence, and hydrate. As a rule of thumb, use the 80/20 rule for your eating choices: eat nutritious foods 80 percent of the time and have a serving of your favorite treats the other 20 percent. For example, eat home-cooked meals 80 percent of the week and enjoy a sensible dinner out on the weekends or a social night with friends (see the sidebar "Macronutrient Primer," page 156). Eating like an athlete will improve how you play, how quickly you recover, and how you feel on and off the court.

BASIC PRINCIPLES

EAT WHOLE FOODS

Choose seasonal, unprocessed whole foods. It's not as easy as it sounds to eat real food. We are surrounded by fast and overly processed foods that we know aren't healthy. Likewise, most convenience foods are produced in a large-scale industrial manner and can hurt not only your health but also the environment. We understand habits are hard to change, and our relationship with food is complex and emotional. Start by adding one whole food choice at a time. Choose a food you like but just don't eat regularly enough. Maybe it's broccoli.

LOCAL AND ORGANIC

Grocery stores all carry organic produce, but so do local farmers' markets. Small local farms may not be certified organic because of the high cost of certification, but they still practice sustainable, pesticide-free farming. This makes them a good choice. Local eggs may be pasture raised, and the chicken and meats may be grass-fed and humanely raised. This farm-to-table shopping gives you produce that's picked fresh and ripe and processed locally, instead of being shipped a long distance.

A good shopping guide for organic versus conventional foods are the Dirty Dozen and the Clean 15 guidelines from the Environmental Working Group (EWG). Every year EWG releases its Dirty Dozen list—the most highly sprayed and chemical-laden crops, foods that you should instead buy organic. Avoiding those toxins in your body is well worth the higher cost of organic produce.

DIRTY DOZEN AND CLEAN 15

THE DIRTY DOZEN
Try to always buy organic or local.

Strawberries	Apples
Spinach	Grapes
Kale, collard, and mustard greens	Bell and hot peppers
Peaches	Cherries
Pears	Blueberries
Nectarines	Green beans

THE CLEAN 15
These are safer to buy nonorganic.

Avocados	Kiwi
Sweet corn	Cabbage
Pineapple	Mushrooms
Onions	Mangoes
Papaya	Sweet potatoes
Sweet peas (frozen)	Watermelon
Asparagus	Carrots
Honeydew melon	

PLAN THREE HEALTHY MEALS

Set your menu for breakfast, lunch, and dinner. Your snacking will naturally decrease if you eat a full, well-rounded dinner.

HYDRATE = WATER

Pickleball players need to stay hydrated to maintain optimal performance. Dehydration can lead to decreased coordination, concentration, and endurance. Most pickleball courts are outside in direct sunlight, and people play for multiple hours in the heat. The excitement of the game can distract you from refueling properly, quickly leading to dehydration. Proper nutrition includes consuming adequate amounts of fluids and electrolytes to not only prehydrate but also replace what is lost through sweating. Once you are cramping and dehydrated, it can take days for your cells to repair. And pay attention to the weather. If you are in a hot and humid environment, you need to increase your water and electrolytes. Dehydration can cause:

- Cramping.
- Heat exhaustion.
- Headaches.
- Decreased performance.
- Poor digestion.
- Stomach cramps.
- Poor sleep.

In addition to water, you need electrolytes. These are key minerals such as sodium, potassium, calcium, and magnesium that are essential for our bodies to carry out functions such as muscle contractions and nerve impulses. It's important to add electrolytes to your water on game or training days. You can accomplish this by mixing ⅛ teaspoon of salt into your water and eating sodium-rich foods such as pickles, lox, pretzels, olives, and anchovies. Avoid sugary hydration drinks, carbs, and fruit when you hydrate. Carbs are great, but eat them after you hydrate.

What to Drink and When

- 2 hours before pickleball: 20 ounces of water with electrolytes.
- 15 minutes before pickleball: 8 ounces of water.
- During play: drink during every break in play.
- Playing longer than 1 hour: add 30 to 60 grams of carbohydrates to fluid. This can be a lemonade, Precision Nutrition PF 30, Skratch Labs sport hydration, or some fruit.
- Postgame: 16 to 20 ounces of fluid for every pound lost during playing or training (which is primarily water weight).
- Preload your workout; hydrate 1 hour prior to playing.
- Don't depend on thirst to determine when to drink water.

Avoid water packaged in plastic: this seems impossible but is important. Plastic bottles—even if they claim to be BPA-free—are proven to be an endocrine disrupter, meaning the chemicals that leach into the water from plastics can increase estrogen levels and decrease testosterone. A plethora of other chemicals that are in the water await you as soon as that bottle hits room temperature. Carry your own metal water bottle and fill it with filtered water from your home.

SUPPLEMENT RECOMMENDATIONS

The research is already voluminous about the benefits of supplements. But the literature on many supplements makes claims about improved health, fitness, and performance that are not supported by independent scientific studies. It is hard not to be swayed by such claims. Which supplements are effective and safe, with evidence to back them up? Back to our expert.

> **Sklaver:** *When I work with clients, we start them out on what we consider essential if you're playing a sport like pickleball. Here is my list:*

WHOLE-FOOD MULTIVITAMIN

Not all vitamins are created equal. Whole-food vitamins from sources like Garden of Life, New Chapter, and Kirkland are superior to synthetic ones. They are more bioavailable (easy for your body to absorb), provide a wider range of nutrients, are easier on your stomach, have proven long-term health benefits, and are a more sustainable choice.

FISH OILS

Boost your intake of essential fatty acids (EFAs), primarily omega-6 and omega-3, but especially omega-3, which we don't get enough of in the Western diet. These EFAs will decrease inflammation, lower muscle soreness, and protect your brain. Your joints, skin, eyes, mood, and immune system all benefit from fish oils. Plant food sources of omega-3 include seeds like ground flax, hemp, and chia. Walnuts, edamame, seaweed, and algae are also plant-based options. For vegetarians and vegans who choose to get their omega-3 exclusively from whole-food sources, it's beneficial to take an algae-based DHA /EPA supplement.

FISH OIL PRIMER: WHAT TO BUY AND HOW MUCH TO TAKE

Look for EPA/DHA fish oil from a cold, clean water source with an added antioxidant such as vitamin E or citrus oil to minimize or eliminate "fish burp." Trusted brands have quality fish oils that are sustainably sourced. Easy-to-travel-with capsules are available, as is liquid, which is usually more potent. Look for a dark-colored bottle; avoid clear bottles, which permit UV light to enter and oxidize the oil, turning it rancid. Store the oil in your fridge and buy smaller bottles to prevent it from going bad.

The general population should take 1 gram a day, which is usually one serving, according to the label. Athletes and those recovering from injury, concussion, or chronic inflammation should take therapeutic doses of 3 to 4 grams a day. Studies have shown no increased advantage after 4 grams.

Fish oils are absorbed through fat, so take them along with your highest-fat meal of the day (usually dinner). In addition, food enzymes act as catalysts in the omega-3 and -6 conversions.

PROTEIN POWDERS

Whey isolate, casein, pea protein, soy, etc. support muscle growth, repair, and recovery. Vegans especially need this added protein. Check the label to ensure your protein supplement offers a complete protein (the nine essential amino acids with at least 2.5 grams of leucine per serving). That is the minimum required to start muscle protein synthesis and prevent muscle protein breakdown. A serving of whey protein is about 25 grams, and one of plant-based protein is about 25 grams if leucine is added. If you are using a plant-based protein without added leucine, you will need about 30 percent more than a whey protein.

PROBIOTICS

Live bacteria and yeasts promote our all-important gut health. These microorganisms restore and maintain a balanced and healthy gut microbiome. Your digestive system will thank you, and you might even notice positive impacts on your mind and mood. If you're on antibiotics, probiotics can help replenish the good bacteria that is killed off by the medication. As with other supplements, there are a variety on the market with different ingredients and levels of colony-forming units (CFUs). CFUs are important because they tell you how many bacteria each dose contains. Talk to your doctor, pharmacist, or health-store expert and do your own research to find what's best for you. A typical dose is between 5–10 billion CFUs.

CREATINE

Creatine is a natural substance that occurs in our muscle cells. As you strength train, creatine boosts your energy production by providing more ATP (adenosine triphosphate), the primary source of energy for muscle contraction. The recommended daily dose of 5 grams can increase your power output and strength. Your brain on creatine enjoys memory and other cognitive benefits.

ELECTROLYTES

During intense exercise, the body loses electrolytes through sweat. Replenishing electrolytes such as sodium, potassium, and magnesium can help maintain proper hydration and prevent muscle cramps. A typical dose is 330–550 mg.

COLLAGEN

A primary structural protein in tendons and ligaments, collagen supports their strength and integrity. Collagen aids in the recovery and repair of these connective tissues after injury or intense physical activity. Your bones, skin, and hair all need enough collagen, too. You need 15 to 20 grams of collagen per serving, taken 1 hour before training or match play.

CURCUMIN

Beat back inflammation with this bioactive compound found in turmeric. It may help with exercise-induced inflammation and muscle soreness, enhancing recovery and performance. It is also an antioxidant. Researchers agree on curcumin's anti-inflammatory properties. Make your joints happy. Take 500 milligrams daily with a fat source for best absorption.

MAGNESIUM

Take this essential mineral for the 360 enzymatic reactions that rely on magnesium. Your muscles, bones, heart, nervous system, and blood sugar levels all call on magnesium. Foods such as leafy green vegetables, nuts, seeds, and whole grains contain magnesium, but supplementing helps when you can't get enough from your diet alone. A typical dose is 300 mg.

SUPPLEMENTS THAT HELP PROTECT AGAINST POLLUTION DAMAGE

Besides supporting our body's activity, some supplements can help our bodies deal with air pollution and its effects on our lungs. Some evidence-based supplements to help protect against pollution damage are:

- Vitamin D. Known as the "sunshine vitamin," vitamin D is important for bone health, immune function, and supplement loss of absorption caused by pollution. A typical daily dose is 1,000 IU D with 200mcg K2 daily.

- Vitamin E. Vitamin E is a potent antioxidant that helps protect cell membranes from oxidative damage. It may also protect against skin aging caused by UV radiation. A typical dose is 250–335 mg daily.

- Vitamin A and carotenoids. Vitamin A is another antioxidant that slows the progression of macular degeneration, an age-related vision problem. It also plays a role in maintaining the integrity of the skin and mucosal linings, acting as a barrier against pathogens.

- NAC (N-acetylcysteine) is a mucolytic agent that breaks down mucus and improves respiratory function in conditions like chronic obstructive pulmonary disease (COPD) and bronchitis. When air quality is poor, NAC can help ease breathing and reduce cough and congestion. A typical dose is 600–1800 daily.

PROTECTIVE NUTRIENTS

Protective nutrients provide specific health benefits and protect the body from various diseases or conditions. These nutrients often have antioxidant, anti-inflammatory, or immune-boosting properties that help prevent or reduce the risk of certain health issues. Here is a list of some protective nutrients.

- Vitamin C is a potent antioxidant that helps neutralize harmful free radicals, which can cause oxidative damage to cells and contribute to aging and chronic diseases. It aids the body's synthesis of collagen to maintain healthy teeth, gums, bones, and joints. It promotes the production of infection-fighting white blood cells and supports the immune system by stimulating the activity of white blood cells. A typical dose is 500 mg daily.

- Choline and omega-3 fatty acids contribute to cell membrane health, neurotransmitter synthesis, and liver and heart health.

ANTI-INFLAMMATORY EATING

Sklaver: *An anti-inflammatory diet is a heart-healthy style of eating that is high in antioxidants and includes omega-3 fatty acids, whole grains, lean* *proteins, healthy fats, and spices. It limits the consumption of processed foods, red meats, and alcohol. You've heard of the Mediterranean diet, which is part of an anti-inflammatory lifestyle. Optimally, an anti-inflammatory, balanced macronutrient diet includes 40 percent carbs, 30 percent protein, and 30 percent fat.*

Anti-Inflammatory Foods

- Fatty fishes (wild salmon, tuna, mackerel).
- Olive oil, flaxseed oil, avocado oil, avocados.
- Nuts and seeds (Brazil nuts, walnuts, almonds, cashews, pumpkin seeds).
- Fruit (grapefruit, oranges, strawberries, guava, watermelon, pineapple).
- Berries (pomegranate, goji berries, blueberries, grapes, blackberries, raspberries).
- Dark leafy greens. Spinach, kale, collard greens, and bok choy are all abundant in calcium. The darker the green, the higher in calcium and nutrients.
- Vegetables (beets, carrots, sweet potatoes, bell peppers).
- Shellfish (oysters, mussels, lobster, crab).
- Lean meats (bison, lean beef, chicken, turkey),
- Pasture-raised eggs, tofu.
- Probiotic foods (Greek yogurt, kefir, sauerkraut, pickles).
- Spices (ginger, turmeric, garlic, chili pepper, oregano, basil, raw cacao powder).
- Whole grains and legumes: (chickpeas, edamame, lentils, oats, purple and sweet potatoes, buckwheat, quinoa, beans, seeded or sprouted multigrain breads).
- Fluids (green tea, carrot ginger juice, green juice with no fruit added, matcha tea, water and electrolytes)

Foods to Avoid

- Fried food, candy, junk food—typically low-nutrition, low-fiber ready-to-eat packaged snacks containing added sugar and/or artificial sweeteners and flavoring.
- Processed foods—typically high in unhealthy fats, calories, sugar, and sodium.
- Heavy creams.
- Refined vegetable oils, commonly sunflower, safflower, corn, and soybean oil, which are major sources of omega-6s, too many of which can contribute to inflammation.

- Sugar-sweetened beverages such as soda, bottled sweetened teas, and fruit juice cocktails.

PORTION SIZES AND TIMING

Regarding how much and how often to eat and whether to fast intermittently, we find conflicting answers. Sklaver recognizes our very real nutritional needs and temptations. She recommends eating full meals instead of snacking or fasting. Many people find themselves snacking and/or skipping meals, which gives us fewer nutrients and more, and often low-quality, calories. Eating full, balanced meals is satiating, preventing the desire to snack. Sklaver prioritizes protein first because it is filling and thermogenic. Thermogenic means we burn energy to digest.

She also notes the importance of eating protein about every four hours for optimal muscle growth and strength. Carbohydrates are essential at least one hour before and after a game or workout (more on this below). A protein and carb together are ideal, like peanut butter on whole-grain bread.

As for portion sizes, those vary per person, but some good guidelines are:

Men
> 2 palm-size portions of protein with each meal (lean meats, fish, eggs, tofu, beans, lentils).
> 2 fist-size portions of veggies.
> 2 cupped-hand-size portions of carbs and 2 thumb-size portions of fat.

Women
> 1 palm-size portion of protein with each meal (lean meats, fish, eggs, tofu, beans, lentils).
> 2 fist-size portions of veggies.
> 1 cupped-hand-size portion of carbs and 1 thumb-size portion of fat.

HOW TO BUILD A SMOOTHIE

Making a smoothie is simple and versatile. You can use various ingredients based on your taste buds and nutritional needs. Follow these guidelines for layering your ingredients to make a well-blended smoothie.

Layer 1: Base liquid. Choose 1 to 2 cups dairy or plant-based coconut, oat, or almond milk. Or simply use water. Putting your liquid base in first will help the blade spin powerfully. Add a sweetener, if using, such as honey, maple syrup, or agave syrup.

Layer 2: Powders. On top of the liquid, add your protein powder and/or fiber, such as psyllium husks, to prevent the powders from sticking to the sides or the bottom of the blender.

Layer 3: Soft ingredients. Next, layer in soft foods like yogurt, kefir, nut butter, bananas, oranges, and fresh (not frozen) fruits.

Layer 4: Leafy greens. Spinach, kale, chard, and so forth go on top of the soft foods.

Layer 5: Hard ingredients. Frozen fruits, carrots, apples, and cucumbers will help push the leafy greens and soft fruits into the blades.

Layer 6: Seeds and nuts. Ingredients like flaxseeds, chia seeds, or nuts should be added after the hard ingredients, so they get mixed in and chopped effectively.

Layer 7: Ice or frozen ingredients: If you use ice cubes or frozen ingredients to chill and thicken your smoothie, they should go on top. Their weight will further push the ingredients down.

Note: Many smoothie blenders are designed to have you turn your blender cup upside down on the base to activate the blender. So reverse the layering order to have the blade close to your liquid base and layer. If you notice the blender struggling, you can pause and use a spatula to stir or adjust the ingredients, then continue blending.

LAST BUT NOT LEAST: PREPARE

Healthy eating cannot happen if you don't prepare. Prepare means shopping and keeping essential items on hand. To prepare means to build a healthy food pantry.

PRE-PICKLEBALL SNACK AND DRINK

Eat at least one hour prior to playing or training. A snack before training will give you more energy for fuel. Aim for the snack to include carbs for fuel and protein for muscle-building. If you are playing for 60 minutes, fuel your body with 30 to 60 grams of carbs. After you're done playing, a smoothie will put you on the path of recovery. Here's one possible recovery smoothie.

POST-PICKLEBALL RECOVERY SMOOTHIE

Anti-Inflammatory Turmeric Protein Shake

10 ounces unsweetened coconut milk, almond, hemp, or nondairy alternative milk

1 medium banana (frozen for a thicker texture)

½ tablespoon powdered turmeric

¼ teaspoon cinnamon

1 pinch black pepper, to help with the absorption of the turmeric

25 grams your favorite vanilla-flavored protein powder

1 tablespoon MCT oil or powder, to help with the absorption of the turmeric

10 to 20 grams collagen peptides

OPTIONAL

Honey or mango for extra carbs if you need to refuel after a workout

1 tablespoon acacia powder if you need some extra fiber

INTRAGAME: KEEPING FUELED DURING PICKLEBALL

To refuel as you play or work out, consume 30 to 60 grams of carbs for every hour of play. Try to use items that don't contain added sugar. You might try:

Energy bars, granola bars, fig bars, or pretzels that are low in added sugar.
Dried or fresh fruit.
Applesauce.
All-natural fruit snacks.

THE BASIC PANTRY: SHOPPING LIST

When you shop, think in terms of these categories: dry goods, canned foods, oils, spices, condiments, refrigerated and frozen foods.

A well-stocked pantry for your healthy lifestyle should include a variety of nutritious and versatile foods that can be used to prepare balanced and wholesome meals. Here's your shopping list:

Grains
- Whole grains like brown rice, quinoa, oats, whole wheat pasta, and whole-grain bread.
- Whole-grain flours (e.g., whole wheat flour, almond flour) for baking.

Legumes and Pulses
- Canned or dried beans (black beans, chickpeas, kidney beans, lentils, split peas).

Nuts and Seeds
- Almonds, walnuts, cashews, and other nuts.
- Chia seeds, flaxseeds, pumpkin seeds, and sunflower seeds.

Oils

- Extra-virgin olive oil, avocado oil for cooking.

Nut Butters

- Nut butters (peanut butter, almond butter) without added sugar or unhealthy fats.

Canned Goods

- Canned tomatoes, tomato sauce, and tomato paste (no added sugar or salt).
- Low-sodium vegetable, chicken, and beef broth.
- Canned tuna or salmon (in water).
- Canned fruits (preferably in natural juice rather than syrup).

Spices and Seasonings

- A variety of herbs and spices (e.g., basil, oregano, thyme, cumin, turmeric, cinnamon) to add flavor without excessive salt or sugar.

Condiments and Sauces

- Low-sodium soy sauce or tamari.
- Mustard, hot sauce, and vinegar (for salad dressings).
- Ketchup and low-fat mayonnaise (in moderation).

Baking Essentials

- Baking powder, baking soda, and yeast.
- Natural sweeteners like honey, maple syrup, or stevia (in moderation).

Cereals and Breakfast Foods

- Whole-grain cereal or granola with no added sugar.
- Unsweetened oatmeal or muesli.
- Protein-added cereals.

Healthy Snacks

- Popcorn kernels (for air-popping).
- Cut veggies, mini carrots.

- Fresh fruit.
- Pretzels.
- Nuts.
- Jerky (nitrate-free).

Miscellaneous
- Unsweetened cocoa powder for smoothies or baking.
- Unsweetened almond milk or other unsweetened plant-based milk alternatives.
- Low-sodium soy sauce or tamari for stir-fries and Asian-inspired dishes.
- Herbal teas or green tea.

Refrigerated/Frozen or Fresh Foods
- Whole fruits or frozen fruit (peaches, berries, bananas, pineapple).
- Whole vegetables or frozen vegetables (spinach, kale, green beans).
- Eggs.
- Chicken breast without skin.

RECIPES

CHIA SEED PROTEIN PUDDING

Prep time: 5 minutes

Cook time: Overnight in refrigerator

Serves 4

1 teaspoon cinnamon

4 scoops collagen peptides

4 servings Garden of Life Plant-Based Sport or Whey protein powder of choice

4 cups unsweetened almond milk

4 tablespoons chia seeds

4 tablespoons chopped walnuts

½ cup berries

In a medium mixing bowl, combine the cinnamon, collagen, and protein powder. Add the almond milk, then whisk in the chia seeds. Let sit for 5 minutes, then stir again to redistribute the chia seeds. Cover the bowl and refrigerate for 3 hours or overnight.

Divide into bowls or mason jars and garnish with chopped walnuts and berries. Enjoy! Store covered in the refrigerator for up to 4 days.

Calories 313: Protein 35 g, Carbs 17 g, Fat 15 g, Fiber 8 g

SLOW-COOKER APPLE-CINNAMON OATMEAL

Prep time: 7 minutes
Cook time: 4 hours in slow cooker or 30 minutes on stove
Serves 8

1 cup steel-cut oats
4 cups water
1 large apple, skin on, diced
½ cup cinnamon

Combine all ingredients and cook in the slow cooker on low for 4 hours or on the stove-top for 30 minutes.

VARIATION: OATMEAL WITH ALMOND BUTTER AND EGG WHITES

4 cooked egg whites
1 tablespoon almond butter
¼ cup slow-cooked oats with apples and cinnamon

Blend cooked egg whites and almond butter into slow-cooked oats.

Calories (with egg whites and almond butter) 365: Protein 27 g, Carbs 38 g, Fat 11 g, Fiber 7 g

PESTO PROTEIN PASTA

This high-protein, high-fiber, high-flavor dish is easy to make and loaded with vitamin A and iron for a quick and balanced meal. It's also vegan or vegetarian.

Prep time: 5 minutes
Cook time: 5 minutes
Serves 1

2 ounces Explore Cuisine Organic Edamame Spaghetti

2 tablespoons Le Grand Vegan Garden Pesto

1 cup spinach

½ ounce sliced almonds

¼ cup chopped cilantro (optional)

½ teaspoon grass-fed butter (optional if vegan)

In a medium pan, bring water to a boil, add the pasta to the water, and cook for 3 minutes (be careful not to overcook). Drain the pasta. In a separate pan, combine the pesto, spinach, almonds, cilantro, and butter, if using, over medium heat and cook until spinach cooks down.

Place pasta on a plate and top with sauce.

Calories 363: Protein 26 g, Carbs 22 g, Fat 20 g, Fiber 11 g

BLACK BEAN CHILI–STUFFED SWEET POTATOES WITH GROUND TURKEY

Prep time: 10 minutes
Cook time: 1 hour
Serves 4

4 medium sweet potatoes

1 pound ground turkey

1 tablespoon organic vegetable broth

1 yellow onion, chopped

1 yellow bell pepper, chopped

2 garlic cloves, minced

1½ tablespoons chili powder

1 teaspoon oregano

½ teaspoon cumin

1¾ cups canned cooked black beans, drained and rinsed

¾ cup tomato sauce

⅓ cup water

¼ cup chopped cilantro

Preheat the oven to 400ºF (204ºC) and line a sheet pan with parchment paper. Use a fork to poke a few holes in the sweet potatoes and place them on the baking sheet. Bake for 45 to 50 minutes, until soft.

While the potatoes cook, spray a medium nonstick saucepan with cooking spray and add the ground turkey. Sauté over medium heat until brown and set aside. In a medium pot over medium heat, add the vegetable broth. Add the onion and bell pepper and sauté for 5 to 7 minutes, or until soft. Add the garlic and cook for 1 minute more. Then add the chili powder, oregano, and cumin. Stir to combine. Reduce the heat to low and add the black beans, tomato sauce, and water and cook for 6 to 8 minutes. Stir in the cooked ground turkey.

Remove the sweet potatoes from the oven. Slice each one down the center and stuff with the black bean chili. Top with cilantro. Serve and enjoy!

NOTES

Leftovers: Refrigerate in an airtight container for up to four days.

Additional Toppings: Top with avocado, cheese, sour cream, or yogurt.

Calories 409: Protein 33 g, Carbs 54 g, Fat 9 g, Fiber 14 g

LOW-FAT EGG ROLL IN A BOWL

Prep time: 7 minutes
Cook time: 30 minutes
Serves 4

1 tablespoon avocado oil

1 medium yellow onion, diced

5 green onions, both green and white parts, diced

4 garlic cloves, minced

1 tablespoon peeled and grated ginger

1 pound skinless chicken breast

6 cups coleslaw mix

2 cups bean sprouts

¼ cup coconut aminos

Heat the avocado oil in a pan over medium-high heat. Add the yellow onion, green onion, garlic, and ginger. Cook for 3 to 5 minutes, stirring frequently, until soft.

Cube the chicken, then add it to the pan. Cook for about 7 to 10 minutes, or until cooked through.

Stir in the coleslaw mix, bean sprouts, and coconut aminos. Stir for 5 minutes, or until veggies have softened. Transfer to bowls and enjoy!

NOTES

If you don't have coconut aminos, use tamari or soy sauce instead.

For a vegetarian option, replace the chicken with 4 eggs, scrambled.

Calories 265: Protein 31 g, Carbs 21 g, Fat 8 g, Fiber 6 g

FREEZER BREAKFAST BURRITOS

Prep time: 30 mins
Cook time: 30 minutes
Serves 10

1 tablespoon extra-virgin olive oil

3 garlic cloves, minced

1 cup diced red onion

2 large sweet potatoes, peeled and diced into ½-inch cubes)

2 red bell peppers, chopped

1 tablespoon cumin

1½ teaspoons chili powder

1 teaspoon sea salt

12 large eggs, whisked

1 pound ground turkey

10 Joseph's Low Carb Wraps (Note: Do not substitute brown rice tortillas.)

Preheat the oven to 400ºF (204ºC) and line 2 sheet pans with foil.

In a large bowl, combine olive oil, garlic, red onion, sweet potato, bell peppers, cumin, chili powder, and salt. Toss well and then spread the veggies across the sheet pans in an even layer. Bake in the oven for 30 minutes or until cooked through, gently tossing at the halfway point.

Meanwhile, spray a large skillet with nonstick cooking spray and set over low-medium heat. Pour the whisked eggs into the skillet and continuously stir to scramble the eggs while they cook.

Set aside. In another skillet sprayed with nonstick cooking spray, brown the ground turkey and set aside.

Divide the eggs, the ground turkey, and the roasted veggies evenly between the tortillas and roll into burritos.

Once the burritos are cooled, wrap them in foil, place in a freezer-safe bag, and freeze. See notes for how to reheat.

NOTES

Reheating in the oven: Heat frozen burritos in the oven at 350ºF (177ºC) for 30 minutes (or less if already defrosted), then unwrap and serve. For a crispier wrap, return to the oven for another 10 to 15 minutes.

Reheating in the microwave: Remove the foil from the defrosted burritos and microwave for 1 to 2 minutes (times will vary depending on your microwave).

Make them spicy: Add more chili powder, cayenne pepper, hot sauce, and/or sliced jalapeño.

Serve them with: Greek yogurt, sour cream, feta, tomatoes, avocado, and/or salsa.

Calories 258: Protein 22 g, Carbs 18 g, Fat 12 g, Fiber 6 g

RECOVERY FROM INJURY

The first seven days after injury or surgery are the most important for nutritional consideration. The metabolic demands put on your body to repair tissue are upward of 20 percent more than for a healthy person.

This means you must increase your calories by 15 to 20 percent and have a high daily protein intake. The right food and supplements can increase the speed of your recovery.

After an injury, you may feel as if nothing is in your control, but there is one area that you do have control over—proper nutrition, which can help speed your recovery time. Through proper nutrition, you can decide what is going into your body and help the healing process.

THE HEALING PROCESS–STAGES

Inflammation (Week 1): Blood cells move to the injured area to begin recovery.

Proliferation (Weeks 2 to 4): Tissues grow and regenerate.

Remodeling (Week 4 to 2 Years): Tissues strengthen and permanent tissue generation occurs.

You might find it hard to eat after an injury. Stress, depression, less exercise, and your mental state can decrease your appetite. However, you must continue to fuel your body. Your body is working hard to rebuild, and you want to prevent muscle loss during this time. Try to have small meals every 3 to 4 hours. Drink your nutrients if eating is difficult.

Add the Good to Feel and Play Better: You can make these changes one step at a time. Forget about what you "can't" eat or "shouldn't" drink; instead, add healthy choices. Eating like an athlete will improve how you play and how you feel on and off the court.

15.

THE PICKLEBALL MINDSET

As pickleball players, we recognize the need for physical fitness. But we too often neglect developing the mental side of the game. In the ultra-competitive world of pro sports, where athletes and teams are always looking for an advantage, the mental edge is not undervalued. Having a sports psychologist on your performance team is essential. This chapter will explore proven sports psychology skills and techniques for developing a winning and resilient mindset.

A sports psychologist is like a personal trainer for the mind, teaching you a set of practical skills to prepare you mentally to play at a high level. By harnessing the power of the mind, instead of becoming a victim of your moods and habitual negative thought patterns, you can take your game to a new level.

Your mindset coach is Dr. Patrick Cohn. Dr. Cohn, the founder of Peak Performance Sports, is one of the nation's leading mental performance coaches. With over thirty years of experience in racket sports, Dr. Cohn will introduce you to key mindset skills and deepen your understanding of how your mind affects your game. As you move through this chapter, you will notice that the skills are interconnected. Mental performance coaches work through the fundamental skills of relaxation, honest awareness, mindfulness, and willingness to change habitual patterns and build new positive habits.

The topics and techniques will include:

- Self-Talk.
- Mental Rehearsal: Pre-Play.
- Focus: Target and Tactics.
- Emotion: Know Your Triggers.
- Relaxation: Mind and Body.
- Mental Tough Mindset.
- Cognitive Agility.

SELF-TALK

Most people have an ongoing conversation with themselves throughout the day. This voice in your head is so familiar that you often don't notice it. Self-talk, as a technique, is a way to take control of your thoughts (at least when you're playing pickleball). Self-talk allows you to replace negative thoughts and emotions with positive ones. Dr. Cohn will help you take control of this chatter and teach you how to apply it effectively in practice and during games.

> **Dr. Cohn:** *Athletes tend to be very reactive to what's happening on the court or in practice. They wait and let their confidence happen or not happen. They wait for something positive to occur, making them feel good—like hitting an early point-winner. If players miss a couple of easy shots or hit a bad dink, they can start to struggle mentally, having negative thoughts like "My stroke is off today." To counter this, we use proactive positive self-talk, a form of getting into a confident state of mind.*

When you apply proactive positive self-talk, you get out in front and build your confidence and resiliency, making you less reactive. We train athletes to proactively use self-talk between points and before matches to help keep confidence high.

MENTAL REHEARSAL: PRE-PLAY

Mental rehearsal is the imaginary movie you play in your head. You envision yourself successfully executing specific skills, movements, and game strategies. You tap into the power of imagination. You envision a scene in detail, using all your senses to create a desired outcome.

In the sports world, Jack Nicklaus popularized the technique of mental rehearsal. Before every shot, he visualized the flawless swing, the ball's flight, and the perfect landing. Dr. Cohn refined the practice of mental rehearsal and coined it *pre-play*.

> **Dr. Cohn:** *Take the serve; what do you want to do with the serve? Slice it? Take it deep? Drop it in shallow? What area? You need to know this so you pre-play the shot in your mind. You bring together the target and the tactic to create the movie in your mind. In most cases, you don't have time to do this during a match, so it's best to visualize it ahead of time. The serve is an*

exception. You can pre-play, hitting a deep shot, and keeping your opponent behind the baseline.

Exercise: Pre-Play—Feel It in Your Body

To create a successful mental rehearsal, find a quiet and comfortable space and make sure you will not be disturbed. Before you start, clearly define what skills, techniques, or strategies you want to improve. Here are some guidelines:

1. Close your eyes and take a few deep breaths to relax your mind and body.
2. Visualize the desired performance. Pay attention to details: body movements, skills, and techniques. Create the scene by visualizing the court. Engage all your senses, making the scene realistic.
3. You are the director; use slow motion, close-ups, and the best angles.
4. While visualizing, focus on positive thoughts and emotions. Imagine yourself feeling confident, strong, and in control. This positive mindset will help reinforce positive neural pathways and enhance your performance.
5. Repeat and practice regularly—rehearsal is a skill that improves with practice.

FOCUS: TARGET AND TACTICS

Dr. Cohn: *Essentially, focus is where you put your attention. Let's take the serve. Trust your instincts. You already know the basic actions and motions of the serve. You don't need to think about the movement because it's already there. It could evolve, but what's there today is all you have, so trust it.*

The critical step is to have a target. Your action is to focus on hitting the ball to your target. Most amateurs, some pros, and many college athletes we work with, when asked what you need to focus on to hit a serve, say something like "Bend my knees, get full extension in my shoulder, and follow through." And I say, no, you've done that thousands of times in practice. You don't need to think about that now. Now you need to think about stroking it freely toward your target.

You need to know your target and tactic—the serve you will deliver. When driving a car, do you focus on your gas, brake pedal, and steering? All that becomes intuitive. This lets you concentrate on the road, the other cars, and your destination. Keep it simple: focus on your target and your tactic.

EMOTION: KNOW YOUR TRIGGERS

We've all seen athletes lose their composure. Sometimes these outbursts are dramatic, but often they are suppressed and internalized. The effect is still the same—a negative result on your performance. Pickleball, though friendly and social, is also emotionally charged. It can be the high of hitting a game winner and the disappointment of losing.

Dr. Cohn: *The first step for controlling emotions is identifying triggers. Discover the mistakes that really set you off. Maybe it's hitting your serve out of bounds? Maybe it's setting up an easy slam for your opponent? Maybe hitting a simple ground stroke into the net? It may simply be selecting the wrong play. Recognizing these triggers is the first step. The next step is to have a method to reduce these acute flare-ups.*

SIGH OF RELIEF: REDUCE FLARE-UPS

Andrew Huberman, a groundbreaking neuroscientist with a knack for making the health benefits of cutting-edge science useful for everyday life, teaches a practical method that is useful for reducing emotional flare-ups: the Sigh of Relief.

Huberman answers the question: What are the patterns of breathing that allow for the most rapid reduction in stress level that can be done in real time so that people can adjust their stress while they're still engaging in life?

RELAXATION: MIND AND BODY

This gets us to the concept of relaxation, a foundational technique for all the performance elements. It's more complicated than just taking a deep breath. Acknowledging the fear and releasing it with a breath is a good first step. Progressive relaxation will help you re-center.

PROGRESSIVE MUSCLE RELAXATION

Progressive relaxation is a process of tensing and then relaxing or releasing the muscle you just tensed. The instructions below will guide you through the process step by step. The process should lead you into a deep state of relaxation and help you release stress.

After you have completed the process, you can create a cue word or short phrase that will help bring some of the benefits immediately. Relaxation is a learned skill. The more you practice, the deeper you'll go, and the more effective your cue word or short phrase will prove to be.

Guidelines

- Inhale and tense the muscle for 5 seconds. Release the tension on the exhale. Breathe rhythmically for 15 to 20 seconds as you send a message to the muscle to release. Repeat for each muscle group.

- Concentrate on how the muscles feel when you contract them and release them. Pay attention to areas that are difficult to tense or to release—give them a little extra attention. This will increase your awareness of when you are relaxed and tense. Ease out of the state before you go back into your day. You can do this exercise before bed to help you sleep. Release the tension as you breathe out.

Tensing and Releasing Muscle by Muscle

- Hands and forearms (one arm at a time): Make a tight fist with your hand.
- Biceps (one arm at a time): Bend your arm at the elbow and contract your biceps.
- Forehead and top of your head: Tense the muscles in the forehead and top of your head.
- Nose and cheeks: Squint and wrinkle your nose, tensing the muscles in nose and cheeks.
- Mouth and jaw: Clench your teeth and pull the corners of your mouth back toward your ears (forced smile).
- Throat and neck: Pull your head back and simultaneously pull your chin down (make a double chin).
- Back: Pull your shoulder blades together and down (as if you were standing at rigid attention).
- Chest: Flex your chest muscles.
- Abdominal muscles: Pull your belly button toward your spine and brace your abs like someone is about to punch you.
- Upper legs (one leg at a time): Lift one leg about six inches off the floor and contract your thigh muscles.
- Calves (one calf at a time): Keeping your leg straight, pull your toes toward you, then point your toes, contracting your calf muscles.
- Feet (one foot at a time): Curl your toes and flex your foot.

COGNITIVE AGILITY

Cognitive agility is your ability to shift your thinking toward positive outcomes, as opposed to being stuck in unproductive thinking patterns. It's making a positive pivot when faced with challenges. In short, it's about being mentally tough. Mental toughness is the ability to be resilient in the face of adversity. Having an agile and skilled mindset enables you to quickly overcome obstacles on and off the court.

Brené Brown, one of the owners of the Austin pro team, the ATX Pickleballers, sees mental toughness differently. "The core of mental toughness is actually self-compassion," Brown said. "People who are mentally tough stay mentally tough because they don't slip easily into shame or self-criticism or self-loathing." We'll give you a method and guidelines to rescript for success.

> **Dr. Cohn:** *When I think of mental toughness in sports, I see it as an umbrella term, which encompasses having a good mental game. For most people, mental toughness means if you get knocked down, you get right back up and back in the game. I look at mental toughness in a more expansive way. I think of it as being mentally resilient. Being mentally resilient means you can bounce back after mistakes. You don't let a loud crowd bother you. You learn and grow from a loss, and you don't beat yourself up. To be more mentally resilient means you aren't swayed easily by adversity.*

Let's look at two common adversity challenges—expectations and fear of failure.

EXPECTATIONS

Expectations are the outcomes of a match, which are directly related to how well you will perform. Placing too much emphasis on outcomes can lead to a variety of performance anxiety issues. This is why you often hear athletes say they try not to get too high or too low.

Dr. Cohn: *Once you know your triggers, you have to explore what it is about each one that causes you to respond. Often this happens at an unconscious level, an automatic response, so it's essential to understand why. Most of the time, the emotions boil from not meeting expectations. Expectation is a crucial concept. We define expectations as the unwritten standards or demands that athletes have for their performance.*

If you don't achieve your expectations, you can get frustrated and/or lose confidence. Expectations create pressure and put you in your head. This makes you tight, setting you up for subpar performance. Essentially, expectations set you up for failure before you even start.

It's best to come up with a healthier reaction or interpretation of that mistake to help you keep your composure and replace expectations with manageable objectives. You can create a positive script for these major trigger events. Create awareness of the old script in your head, your old reaction, and then replace it with a more positive and rational response. It's a lot about acceptance that "I'm human, I'm going to make mistakes, and I'm not always going to play up to those expectations."

FEAR OF FAILURE

Dr. Cohn: *Anxiety is often about fear of failure. It comes in many different forms. It could be a fear of embarrassment, of the consequences of losing, of disappointing a partner if you're playing with one, or letting down parents, coaches, or your new love interest. Fear can cause you to avoid challenging situations leading to growth both on the pickleball court and in life. Addressing the fear of failure is crucial for athletes to perform at their best, maintain a positive mindset, and enjoy their sports journey.*

Often fear of failure is what fits under the umbrella of social approval. To address that and help athletes relax, we have to focus on the fears that are creating the tension. We call these the what-ifs. We help alleviate these problems by changing the focus, using tools of self-talk, pre-play, concentrating on tactics and targets. You can also use the technique of rescripting.

ANXIETY AND SOCIAL APPROVAL

We think as we age that social pressure is something that happens when you're a teenager, but it continues in more complex and subtle ways. For many athletes, the source of pregame worry comes from a need to have others "approve" of their game. If this is you, you might have the need to be admired, accepted, respected, or liked by other people. You worry about performing poorly because you think it may influence what others think about you. Thus, if you crave approval from others, you are more likely to become anxious or afraid to fail in competition. Your need for social approval underlies and supports the fear of failure. What happens when you want others' approval but can't get it? Stress! Many people who need outside permission to feel good about themselves are prone to pregame anxiety. The root causes are complex, but fear of failure usually starts when athletes worry about the potential consequences of failure.

Overall, pickleball has its social pressures. There's the period spent waiting for your turn to play. A big crowd at the courts means everyone is watching your game. You might feel a little performance anxiety, even though pickleball is a fun game, not life-and-death. But let's acknowledge the tension. Is pickleball for enjoyment? Is it competitive? Or a combo? Depending on your pickleball community, there can be more or less pressure to perform and more or less judgment. Add to that the pressure we put on ourselves. And this is where your pickleball mindset can come to the rescue.

HOW TO WRITE A NEW SCRIPT

You can follow these steps for writing new scripts for challenges of dealing with your emotions, expectations, social pressure, and fear of failure.

Exercise: Bounce Back from Mistakes

1. Identify and list your top 5 triggers.
2. Describe your reaction to the trigger. For example, if you hit a return into the net, what do you think to yourself? Maybe: "I should never hit a return that bad. This is unacceptable."
3. Interpret each trigger. Evaluate your current behavior and its impact on your game and your life. Recognize any patterns or triggers associated with the behavior to understand it better.
4. Replace this reaction and interpretation with a new script. The new script: "I'm not perfect. Even the pros miss shots into the net. Move on to the next point."
5. Use affirmations to reinforce your commitment and boost your belief in yourself.
6. Be kind to yourself during this process. Acknowledge that setbacks are normal and use them as learning opportunities to refine your approach.
7. Monitor your progress. Establish a system to track it regularly. Keep a journal, use a habit-tracking app, or find an accountability partner.
8. Celebrate your achievements and your progress along the way. Recognize and reward yourself for reaching milestones, no matter how small they may seem.
9. Review your script regularly, and periodically make any necessary adjustments to it. Update your goals and strategies as needed to continue moving forward.
10. Seek the support of others. Consider sharing your script with a trusted friend, family member, or mentor who can provide encouragement and can help keep you accountable.
11. Follow your script consistently. Remember that behavior change takes time, patience, and persistence.

Having a new, more effective response to each trigger helps you stay composed.

IT'S A PROCESS
(LIKE EVERYTHING WORTHWHILE)

Dr. Cohn's philosophy and methods can help take you to an optimal flow state, immersing you in the moment with full focus and ease. This state can lead to a heightened awareness that can result in a peak experience of mind, body, and spirit. Beyond sports, building mindset skills gets to the essence of how you create change—by transforming the way you think. Because it's a skill, not a quick fix, you have to work at it, just as you work to develop your game and physical skills through training. Taking a proactive approach to build your mindset will have payoffs on and off the court.

16.

YOUR PICKLEBALL
SPORTS MEDICINE TEAM

A TEAM MEETING

The media is saturated with stories about the epidemic of pickleball injuries. Even health insurance companies are calling it a crisis, with estimates that pickleball injuries will cost them up to $400 million in 2023. For most of us, going to the doctor is no fun. And depending on your insurance and deductible, it can also be expensive.

In this chapter, our medical specialists will look at how the PB-150 program works synergistically to keep you healthy and performing at your potential.

Your medical team offers advice if you get hurt, helping you recover from minor tweaks, strains, and sprains. Even better, they will offer suggestions on how to stay pain-free.

Meet the Medical Team

Dr. Joshua Dines, a sports medicine specialist and the medical director for Major League Pickleball, will give you a framework for thinking about injuries.

Will Sevening, the legendary and longtime athletic trainer for the San Antonio Spurs, will guide you through managing and healing the inevitable sprains, strains, and tweaks. He will offer specific steps to follow before you return to the court.

Dr. Daniel Laby and Dr. Keith Smithson, our sports vision experts, will provide methods to keep your eyes healthy and functioning at performance level.

Peggy Brill, author and physical therapist extraordinaire, will share her concept of instant relief and give you some moves you can do right on the court to relieve pain and play on.

YOUR SPORTS MEDICINE EXPERT: DR. JOSHUA DINES

Athletes of all levels dedicate significant time and effort to their sport. However, injuries can still occur even with conscientious preparation and training. A sports medicine doctor can help give you a framework for deciding how to most effectively deal with an injury. As a result, you return to the court as quickly and safely as possible.

INTRODUCTION: WHAT IS SPORTS MEDICINE?

Dr. Joshua Dines has spent his career helping elite athletes get back in the game at their full potential after an injury. His experience treating professional athletes stems from his work as a team doctor for the New York Mets, the New York Rangers, the U.S. Davis Cup tennis team, and the Los Angeles Dodgers. As a sports medicine physician and orthopedic surgeon at New York's Hospital for Special Surgery (HSS), Dr. Dines is in a unique position to evaluate nonsurgical and surgical solutions. Under the umbrella of sports medicine, he is trained to diagnose, treat, and manage sports injuries to the musculoskeletal system and correct underlying conditions that can negatively affect your physical performance.

Q: Why Major League Pickleball?

Dr. Dines: *I became the medical director for Major League Pickleball not just to help the pickleball pros but to better understand the physical challenges affecting pickleball players of all levels and gain a deeper insight on how to keep them healthy. Ultimately, to also be a source of information for the recreational PB community. We see a lot of pickleball patients at HSS, and we want to constantly expand our knowledge regarding the best treatment methods. I've done a lot with tennis medicine for the Davis Cup team and high-ranked players, so pro pickleball seemed like a natural fit.*

Q: When it comes to injuries, is there a framework that pickleball players can use to help them better understand how to think about them and make intelligent choices?

Dr. Dines: *From a big-picture perspective, injuries fall into two categories: acute and chronic. On a spectrum, any injury can go from acute to chronic if they aren't treated properly. Ankle sprains are an example of an acute injury. While ankle sprains are common, one can decrease the chance of sustaining a sprain by being in shape and building up mobility and stability in the ankle joint. If an injury does occur, not doing too much too quickly after an injury will hopefully prevent minor, acute injuries from becoming more chronic. While all ankle sprains aren't the same, the overwhelming majority of them will get better in a week or two with a little ice, anti-inflammatories, and rest. Usually, if you tweak your ankle, but you can hobble off the court, and you put some ice on it and by later that day you're feeling a little better, or a day or two later, you're feeling pretty good, probably not a big deal. A key point is realizing that while most injuries will get better, some may be more severe and warrant further work-up. When do you go for treatment? When do you go for more advanced treatment, non-operative, from a sports doctor or an orthopedic surgeon?*

Suppose you're still limping after a couple of days. In that case, or if you're having difficulty putting weight on it, or if you felt a pop or a tear, those are signs that something more serious happened. In these cases, it's worth getting looked at to ensure you're not missing a more severe injury that could require advanced imaging or more intensive treatments. Another criterion: Has the pain stopped you from playing for more than a week or two? And if it's affecting not just pickleball but wakes you up at night, it's hard walking up and down stairs, and the limp lingers just getting around the house, all of these are signs that there's probably something more going on.

You don't want to take something that would heal well by recovering conservatively and overdo it. Play on it more, beat it up, and now you've changed the spectrum of what needs to be done. And you're talking about surgery or a much longer recovery for something that would've gotten better with conservative treatment. The same is true with other joints: your knee, rotator cuff, and elbow. If you feel a rip or a tear, you should go to a doctor. Those are the ones you want to stay ahead of regarding having them worked up appropriately. This doesn't necessarily mean you need surgery, but at least get it looked at. The doc may say anti-inflammatories and/or formal physical therapy are all you need. This is the best way to avoid surgery.

Q: How do the various body areas work synergistically?

Dr. Dines: *It's also important to get your full range of motion back. If you don't, it can have an effect up or down what we call the kinetic chain. This is the key concept. You could be hitting a volley, a ground stroke, or an overhead. While it's your shoulder and arm delivering the most visible action, the action really starts with your feet, ankles, knees, and hips; then it goes up through your core, through your whole body. This entire chain is what generates the energy and the power. If you have an ankle sprain, you're not putting full weight on it, or your range of motion is a bit compromised, this means you're not pushing it with sufficient ground force. All of a sudden, other things work a little differently to compensate. This is where small things lead to bigger things if they need to be addressed appropriately and initially.*

Q: Why is it important for pickleball players to train for the game?

Dr. Dines: *The biggest point I make with pickleball players is you both need to be in shape and not overdo it. Many players start to play, and it's so fun that they want to be out there for hours. It seems relatively easy on the body because it's not as demanding as playing singles tennis for an hour. But if you're not properly warming up, combined with a lot of standing and sitting between games, that's a pretty good recipe for an injury. Along those lines, pickleball should not be your only form of exercise. Working out to build up strength, improving your cardiovascular* *health, and playing different sports will all help prevent injuries while playing pick-leball.*

Q: How essential is it to strengthen your rotator cuff?

Dr. Dines: *The stronger your rotator cuff and scapular are, the better they can stabilize, and the better chance you have of preventing injury or recovering more quickly from injury.*

Q: What can you do to protect against an Achilles injury?

Dr. Dines: *Four years ago, I tore my Achilles playing tennis. There are some preventative signs, but they are very subtle. I was at a tennis tournament, and I did more than usual in preparing to play, and it still happened to me. My advice is, if you do feel something back there or if you get a calf strain, it makes sense to take it easy and let that pain calm down instead of rushing back. Remember, the better the shape you're in if an injury happens, the easier your comeback will be.*

As medical director of Major League Pickleball, Dr. Dines stresses the importance of a fitness program to decrease injuries. He also knows you can do everything right and still get hurt. If this happens, be kind to yourself on your road to recovery and return to play.

YOUR ATHLETIC TRAINER: WILL SEVENING

In the world of sports, athletes are always looking for ways to get an edge over the competition. They work tirelessly to improve their skills, strength, and endurance. However, no matter how much athletes train, injuries are inevitable in any sport. That's where athletic trainers come in—to help prevent, diagnose, and treat injuries.

Will Sevening has been a key part of the San Antonio Spurs culture since 1998. He was the athletic trainer for all five of their NBA championships and has worked with elite Hall of Famers and mentored young players over the last twenty-six years. He was the Western Conference head athletic trainer at the 2016 NBA All-Star Game and served as an athletic trainer for the 2019 USA Basketball National Team.

Q: What is the role of an athletic trainer?

Sevening: *We come into public awareness when there's an injury during a game. But we do more than treat acute injuries. We try to prevent injuries and minimize the effects of typical aches and pains. Education is one of the biggest components, one that often flies under the radar. I educate and empower the athlete. This is especially important in the off-season, when we're not around them daily. For the recreational pickleball player, this is even more vital because you're most likely not going to have regular access to a trainer.*

My goal is to help athletes know what they can do to prepare for a game and know the limitations of the body, and to give them simple tools for recovery and ways to eliminate the wear and tear that playing creates. If you play hard or play a lot, you'll get sore. This is not a bad thing; you just don't want the effects to accumulate in a negative way.

Q: What are some self-assessment questions for a player to ask?

Sevening: *Take the following scenario. You're stepping onto the pickleball court with some challenges: a previous injury that's caused compensations, a poor fitness level due to inactivity, and a genetic issue (one leg slightly shorter than the other). This is normally a small problem when navigating daily activities: shopping, housework, and traveling for vacation. But now you're an athlete, moving with more speed, power, and changes of direction than life. These manageable body challenges can turn into injuries. Pickleball players often don't think that way. They're out to play and have fun. So the first step is an assessment of areas you need to work on. You need to understand where you are athletically.*

- **What is your experience as a player?** Are you a beginner or an intermediate or advanced player? If you are a beginner, are you a first-time player? If so, you should start slow. It's going to take some time for your muscles and joints to adapt. If you are an intermediate or an advanced player, these movements aren't new to you, but now you're going to be playing at a higher level and putting more intense athletic demands on your body.

- **What is your fitness level?** You can be a high-level player without putting in time and effort for conditioning and strength training. If pickleball is your only source of fitness training, you could be at an increased risk of injury.
- **Do you have any physical limitations?** Genetic (like scoliosis), or from previous injuries or medical conditions?
- **How old are you?** It's important to think about being an athlete throughout your lifespan.

PB-150 helps you clean up some of your deficits with a prehab routine, makes sure you are warmed up dynamically, improves the strength of your major movement patterns, and gives you a cooldown to improve your range of motion and release your muscles.

Q: What is the pickler's most important piece of training equipment?

Sevening: *Shoes and socks. The famous Michael Jordan/Spike Lee commercial held a lot of truth for athletic trainers. It's important to have the right shoe, and a high-quality shoe is crucial. This is crucial to help minimize injuries, especially if*

MIND YOUR FEET

When you're walking around the house barefoot, take some time to be mindful of your feet. We tend to forget about their full function—how they can flex and extend. Working and increasing this capacity will improve your balance and movement.

Towel Grabs: These are simple exercises for working the foot muscles in flexion. You put a towel on the floor, and while you are flexing your toes toward your heels, you grab the towel and pull it (crinkling it) toward your heel.

Towel Spread: Now work it the opposite way: you extend your toes out and push the towel away. This brings your toes into extension.

Big Toe Down: Press your big toe down to the floor, as you raise your other four toes in the air.

Big Toe Up: Raise your big toe up as your other four toes press down into the floor.

---

you're starting to log much time on the court. You will be doing a lot of lateral cutting and quick stops and starts, so a mid-cut shoe or one designed for tennis would be a good choice.

Q: What are the best ways to use hot and cold treatments?

Sevening: *You can warm up a sore or vulnerable area with moist heat, a hot pack, or a heating pad. Heat warms up tendons, joints, and tight muscles. It also helps increase blood flow and gets oxygen to the muscles. You can use a towel, a T-shirt, or rolled-up paper towels as a protective layer to prevent burning. Applying the heat for 10 to 20 minutes will be beneficial. An analgesic balm (a topical that provides penetrating warmth) is also an option. Ice will help reduce swelling and inflammation. You can use a cold pack or ice wrapped in plastic or in a towel, or create an ice massage cup. To make an ice massage cup:*

- Get a paper cup.
- Fill it with ice or water.
- Freeze it and then tear off the top part of the cup, so that the ice is exposed and you still have a place to hold the cup.
- Apply the ice in a targeted way to the chosen area.

If you're using ice packs, keep them in the area for 20 minutes. As far as the lateral part of the knee and elbow, stop the session if you get a tingling down the fingers or foot. If you have access to a cold tub, those help with the buildup of lactic acid.

Q: What do you do when an injury happens?

Sevening: *Mindset support is a big part of my job, too. I can't change the fact that an athlete got hurt, so we have to help them accept it and encourage them to move on and attack their rehab with the same fervor they have for playing the game they love. Okay, an injury happens. Where do we go from here? We set our goals and have little victories on our way. Your PB-150 combine tests are a good way to determine if you're ready to return to the court. According to BAM protocols, you should be able to perform the tests pain-free.*

YOUR SPORTS VISION EXPERTS: DR. DANIEL LABY AND KEITH SMITHSON

SPORTS VISION DEFINED

Have you ever had trouble tracking the pickleball as it moves across the net? Do you feel like your hand and eye coordination could be better? Vision training is vital. Sports vision training can enhance hand-eye coordination, depth perception, tracking ball movement, and visual reaction time.

Your first coach for sports vision, Daniel M. Laby, MD, began his work in the field more than three decades ago with the Los Angeles Dodgers, and currently works with almost a third of all MLB teams, has worked with several NBA and NHL teams, and has worked with teams at two Olympics. He has published over a dozen research papers on sports vision, and his work has been recognized by the American College of Sports Medicine and the American Optometric Association, Sports Vision Section. Dr. Laby also hosts a YouTube channel with over eleven thousand subscribers and consults with MLB as well as Premier League players in the UK.

Q: What is your approach to sports vision training?

Dr. Laby: *I ensure my athletes have a strong base for their visual system. These elements include visual acuity and the classic eye exam. Twenty-twenty vision is often considered the standard. For pickleball, I would recommend trying to correct your vision to twenty-fifteen, using corrective lenses, under your ophthalmologist's supervision. You need sharp enough vision to pick up the spin on the ball and pick up racket orientation that will impact where the ball goes. Additionally, you need fast reactions of your hands and feet and excellent hand-eye coordination, among other abilities. After you've cleared the basic eye exam, there are basic exercises to help you on the pickleball court.*

Q: How do eye exercises work?

Dr. Laby: *They involve neuroprocessing, which is decision-making. It's how your* brain puts together the data from your eyes. You're at the kitchen line, and the ball is coming at you. You have to react. Your motor reaction must be perfectly timed with the right speed and strength. A lot of visual information gets translated into hand-eye coordination. It involves fast reaction, timing, and coordination to make a successful move.

The purpose of the visual system is to anticipate the future. If you can correctly anticipate the future, you will be very successful. Those are the two critical components we want to train. It's what Wayne Gretzky once said: "I don't skate to the puck. I skate to where the puck is going to be."

Vision is not physical; it's cognitive, so the exercises for improving your vision on the court are about improving cognitive efficiency. The eyes are simply receivers. But the real crux of vision is what happens in the brain. It's different from learning how to use your hands or your feet.

Q: Could you explain the concept of quiet eye?

Dr. Laby: Quiet eye is an important concept. It can be defined as what you look at just before, during, and after a sport's skill is critical. Dr. Joan Vickers in Calgary, Canada, initially discovered this phenomenon. The technique has three parts. In pickleball, you'd see the ball just prior to making contact with the paddle, the ball making contact, and maintaining eye fixation on that point for a moment after the contact. This focus triggers other physiological effects. When you employ the quiet eye, your heart rate tends to decrease, and there's better muscle movement—that adds to more success. Quiet eye can also be helpful in times of increased stress, and fortunately it can be trained!

THE SPORTS VISION PRO

Your second coach, Keith Smithson specializes in sports vision for improved performance. He is the cofounder of Sports Vision Pros and currently the director of visual performance for the Washington Nationals and Washington Commanders and the founder of Sports Vision Pros. The mission of Sports Vision Pros (SVP) is to connect the worlds of sports and vision. The SVP trainers help athletes of all ages perform at their best to enjoy and continue playing sports. Smithson has prepared a pregame warm-up to add to your PB-150 training lineup.

THE SPORTS VISION PROS PICKLEBALL PREGAME WARM-UP

This warm-up involves spending 3 to 5 minutes on each of four different drills to warm up the relevant visual skills needed for effective pickleball.

NEAR/FAR FOCUS

PURPOSE
This drill works on eye teaming and the near-far focusing mechanism for athletes.

SETUP
The athlete picks out words on their paddle or creates a target with a permanent marker.

THE DRILL
The athlete shifts focus between the near target seen on their paddle when held at arm's length and a target in the distance:

> A doorknob across the room.
> An object on a bookshelf.
> A pickleball placed on the other side of the net.

During the task, the athlete gradually brings the near point (paddle target) closer to their eyes to increase difficulty.

TARGET BALL TRACKING

PURPOSE
This is an eye-tracking and eye-hand coordination drill.

SETUP

The athlete takes a standard pickleball and mark on opposite sides of the ball two red circle targets with a permanent marker, then two black triangles and two blue plus signs
(or other contrasting colors, depending on the ball color).

THE DRILL

The athlete and a partner start 14 feet apart (distance from kitchen line to kitchen line).
Before each paddle contact, the athlete calls out the symbol on the ball.

To increase difficulty, picklers can move closer to their partner, or closer to a wall if
warming up or practicing alone. This decreases the time to identify the symbols on
the ball targets.

Note: Avoid using red and green targets if the athlete has congenital color blindness.

BODY ZONES:
TRACKING AND TIMING

PURPOSE

Warm up and improve smooth tracking in central and peripheral gaze at three levels,
train anticipatory timing, and tune vision into the rebound speed of the pickleball.

SETUP

A pickleball.

THE DRILL

Using your dominant hand, bounce the pickleball directly in front of you, then to the
outside your left foot, and outside your right foot. Bounce the ball in the three positions and catch it at knee level, catching it at the apex of the bounce.

Bounce the ball in the three positions and catch it at waist level, catching it at the apex
of the bounce.

Bounce the ball in the three positions and catch it at shoulder level, catching it at the apex
of the bounce.

Your goal is to not move your head, just your eyes, arms, and hands.

Think of trying to grab the ball from above (like a skill claw), at the peak of the bounce.

If you are tall, you may need to squat down to have the balls bounce higher into your visual field, since pickleballs don't easily bounce high.

Try using your left hand to throw the ball for your left foot and your right hand for your right foot.

SOLO PADDLE BALL BOUNCE

BENEFIT

Enhances hand-eye coordination.

EQUIPMENT

Pickleball paddle and pickleball.

THE MOVE

Toss the ball in the air and hit it with your paddle, bouncing it back up. Try to hit the middle of the paddle (the sweet spot) for each contact and call out the symbol on the ball before you make contact.

For added challenges:

> You can flip the paddle each time.
>
> Make each hit challenging to return (you have to move your feet to get to the ball and/or make a challenging reach). After you hit the ball, close your eyes and open them quickly to find the ball.

DURING YOUR WORKOUT

EXERCISE

Toss and catch with movement patterns.

THE MOVE

Perform the following toss-and-catch variations with your marked pickleball while doing the following exercises.

VARIATIONS

Toss a ball in the air and catch it with the same hand.

Toss a ball in the air and catch it with the other hand.

EXERCISES

Front lunge.

Back lunge.

Lateral shuffle.

Carioca.

UPGRADES

Call out the number on the pickleball before you catch it.

Close your eyes and toss, then track and catch as you execute the movement pattern.

PAIN-FREE PICKLEBALL

We all will deal with aches and pains. Because pickleball pushes the body beyond the norms of daily activity, pickleball players of all ages can develop pain. Pro athletes have the advantage of a team PT to help them get on top of pain early—and now you have one on your team, too.

Peggy Brill, PT, founder of Brill Physical Therapy, board member for New York's Hospital for Special Surgery Rehabilitation Network, and author of the books *Instant Relief* and *The Core Program,* has made it one of her missions to help people live a pain-free life. In the sports world, she has worked with athletes of all levels, including the legendary Duke basketball team under Coach K.

One of her specialties is the concept of instant relief. In recent years, Brill has turned her attention and expertise to pickleball and has developed easy-to-do exercises that address common pickleball injuries. Based on a sound understanding of anatomy and physiology, these evidence-based instant relief exercises reduce common pickleball aches and pains.

Brill: *When it comes to your pickleball body, I've seen the gamut, both upper and lower extremity injuries. It's important to delineate where the problem is coming from versus just treating the symptom. The instant relief method offers dozens of exercises to address the root causes of pain. For the pickleball player, I want to offer two powerful moves, one for the upper body and one for the lower body, that can help with a variety of potential issues.*

Q: Your exercise, the Brill Chicken, is a powerful thing of beauty. What are the benefits?

Brill: *It was the catalyst for my book* Instant Relief. *The exercise elongates tightened pectorals, strengthens the upper back muscles that control the shoulder blades, and stretches the neck muscles to decompress lower neck segments—all at the same time. And it can be done right on the court for a quick reset. You can do these two practical moves before you play, during, and after.*

Q: What are the benefits of the piriformis stretch?

Brill: *This is a powerful lower body move for your hips and helps relieve sciatic nerve pain, which is common. It also involves rotation, which complements the Brill Chicken with a different movement pattern that activates trunk rotation.*

EXERCISES

🎾 BRILL CHICKEN

ON-THE-COURT PICKLEBALL POINTERS

This exercise is important for pickleball because it maximizes the strength and power of the upper extremities. You can do this movement sitting or standing, before you play, between points or between games, or when you're done for the day.

Pain cues to prompt this move: tingling, shooting pain, numbness, tightness a knot, a pinch, ache, a burn, limited range of motion without pain, fatigue, and weakness.

THE MOVE

Tuck in your chin and pull your head back, elongating the back of your neck. Push out your chest and lift it, pinching your shoulder blades together. Bend your arms and pull your hands back toward your shoulders, keeping your elbows close to your torso and your palms facing outward. Hold for a count of 10, and release.

🏓 HOME PROGRESSION: BRILL PRONE CHICKEN

ON-THE-COURT PICKLEBALL POINTERS

To get ahead of shoulder pain at home before or after you hit the court, build on the Brill Chicken by doing it from the prone position. In this lying-down variation, you get all the benefits of the standing version, with the bonus of strengthening your upper back by resisting gravity. This will result in greater back strength and better posture when you sit upright.

THE MOVE

Lie on your stomach. Tuck in your chin and pull your head back to elongate the back of your neck. Push out your chest and pinch your shoulder blades together. Bend your arms, keeping the elbows close to your torso with your wrists pulled back and the palms facing away from your head.

Raise your head, chest, and arms off the floor or bed, hold for a count of 10, and gently release.

🏓 STANDING PIRIFORMIS STRETCH

ON-THE-COURT PICKLEBALL POINTERS

This exercise is important for pickleball because it frees the hips to rotate around the pelvis and opens the vertebrae in the lumbar spine, which prevents strains. You can do this movement sitting or standing, before you play, between points or between games, or when you're done for the day.

Pain cues to prompt this move: tingling, shooting pain, numbness, tightness a knot, a pinch, ache, a burn, limited range of motion without pain, fatigue, and weakness through lower extremities.

THE MOVE

With your legs shoulder width apart, stand a foot away from a chair (or other surface you can hold on to), positioning yourself so that the side that hurts is next to the chair.

Holding on to the chair for balance, bend and raise that knee. Using the opposite hand, pull the knee across your body so that the side of the hip gets a good stretch. Keep the standing leg and hip stationary.

Hold the position for a count of 10 and then repeat with the other leg.

YOUR SPINE ON PICKLEBALL

THE IMPORTANCE OF THE SPINE

The spine consists of 33 vertebrae, connected by ligaments and intervertebral discs. It runs from the base of your skull to the tailbone. This structure has two functions: to allow movement and to protect the spinal cord's billions of nerve fibers. These nerves carry messages back and forth between the brain and the body, allowing us to function in all our magnificence. Happy spine, happy life.

Back pain can dramatically affect your pickleball lifestyle if you don't take a proactive approach. Fortunately, pickleball can help you beat the odds and be a portal into restoring spine health. Understanding how your spine is structured and how it is designed to function can improve your game on the court and keep you pain-free.

YOUR SPINE'S THREE-PART STRUCTURE

Your spine has three sections: the lower, also called the lumbar; the middle spine, also called the thoracic; and the upper spine, called the cervical (the neck). The spine can move in all directions—forward and backward, side to side, and in rotation. When it comes to pickleball, your spine has a pickleball personality—things it likes to do on the court and things it doesn't like to do. Each of the three areas has its strengths and weaknesses. Let's look at the spine one section at a time.

Your spine health coach is Bryon Holmes. Holmes has spent his life helping people keep their lower backs healthy. Holmes holds a master's in exercise physiology and sports science from the University of Florida. His master's thesis and his continued research focus is on back health. As cofounder of MedX, the holistic physical therapy and fitness center in Estes Park, Colorado, Holmes worked extensively with retirees who moved to Colorado to pursue an active lifestyle in sports, fitness, and outdoor activities.

LOWER BACK (THE LOWEST FIVE VERTEBRAE)

Holmes: *Your lower spine is built for the dink. It's designed to move forward and backward (flexion and extension), similar to your dinking motion. A strong lower back will help you dink with more precision and dink all day long. The lower back can rotate, but with a limited range of motion. Of all three segments, the lumbar has the least ability to rotate. If asked to rotate through a large range of motion, it will not be happy. The inevitable outcome will be pain. If you've ever suffered lower back pain, you know how intense and debilitating this can be. Building strength in your lower back will allow you to play at a higher level and pain-free for a lifetime.*

MIDDLE BACK (THE TWELVE MIDDLE VERTEBRAE)

Holmes: *This area centers around your shoulder blades—above your lower back and below your neck. Your middle back can bend forward and backward like the lower back, but unlike the lower back, it has a limited range in this plane of motion. Also unlike the lower back, it can rotate through an impressive range of motion. This rotation is critical for performing forehands, backhands, and the volley game. Many of us have lost mobility in our lumbar spine. We are slumped and rounded from texting, sitting in front of our computers, or bingeing on TV shows. When this hunched shape becomes habitual, the middle back loses its ability to rotate, which is one of its primary* functions. *Stuck in a rounded position, the middle back also loses its ability to move backward and lengthen into extension. This decreases healthy movement and alignment.*

As you play pickleball or engage in daily activities with a rounded posture, the lower back is forced to compensate. It takes on rotational duties, which it is not designed to do, especially with the repetitive and intense demands of pickleball. This compensation will eventually lead to lower back pain and injury. You may get by in life with a limited range of middle back motion, but on the court, when you're swinging and rotating powerfully, the wear and tear on your lower back will eventually lead to pain and potentially more serious injuries. For this part of your spine, think of gently lengthening and initiating rotational movements from between your shoulder blades.

NECK (THE SEVEN UPPER VERTEBRAE)

Holmes: *Your neck, of the three segments, has the largest range of motion in all directions. Like the middle back, through texting, our neck is challenged. Forward head posture has become an epidemic. Your neck, head, and eyes are the critical leaders of a movement. In sports, we've all been told, "Keep your eye on the ball." If you can't turn your head, you will have to turn your whole body, putting it in a less optimal position for generating power and at risk of injury. Your eye's ability to see and detect movement will be hindered if the neck cannot move freely through its range of motion. Or if the neck moves out of its optimal zone of movement to compensate for an immobile middle spine, you may experience chronic neck soreness or get injured.*

THE UNGUARDED MOMENT

Holmes: *In sports, you expose yourself to the unguarded moment. These are moments when you suddenly react to a situation you were not expecting or couldn't easily predict. These spontaneous improvised moments are also the beauty of sports. You go from a dink to rotating and turning for an overhead slam. If your spine is strong and flexible, your chances of injury* *decrease dramatically. Injuries are more likely to occur during an unguarded moment.*

GUARDING

Holmes: *The opposite is guarding, which is the body's response to pain. The guarding pattern protects injured areas by not using the muscles that activate it, creating a new pattern of firing to compensate. This causes the injured area to stay weak and deconditioned, increasing the chances of reinjuring, or leading to chronic pain.*

A HAPPY PICKLEBALL SPINE

For your spine to be happy, all three areas must have the functional flexibility and strength to do their job. Knowing how each area functions will improve both your awareness and use. When you're warming up, focus on:

Using the flexion and extension motion of your lower back when you dink.
Rotating and extending through your middle back for your forehand and
    backhand, avoiding a rounded, turtleback posture.
Moving your neck freely and keeping your eye on the ball.

As you implement this spine awareness in your warm-ups, it will make its way into your game.

A healthy spine comes from increasing its strength, improving its mobility, and mindfully using it the way it is designed. All of this will make your spine athletic and help you avoid unnecessary wear and tear through misuse. Pickleball can be an opportunity to restore and build a healthy spine.

THE PICKLEBALL WELLNESS
WARM-UP DANCE

In sports and fitness, dance and dance metaphors often enter the mix. Aerobics classes often become popular because of the way they're choreographed. Some Madonna videos look like exercise classes. The details that athletes choreograph into their celebrations after a score look more like dance than sport. Athletes are often called balletic and graceful. Dancers are often described as strong and athletic. Like fitness and sports, dance breaks are a great form of physical activity to proactively counter the sedentary lifestyle. Dance improves your agility, balance, coordination, mood, and cognitive functioning. As practiced in this section, it will also improve you pickleball game. Is it a dance or a warm-up? It's both.

UNDERSTANDING THE THREE
BASIC MOVEMENT PATTERNS

In the exercise science world, the specializations of biomechanics and kinesiology study how the body moves. They break it down into three planes of motion: the sagittal, the frontal, and the transverse. These are the academic terms you'd memorize for a test. Let's apply them to pickleball.

Simply put, the body moves forward and backward (sagittal plane), side to side (frontal plane), and in rotation (transverse plane). The body mixes and matches these building blocks to create an infinite variety of movements. In pickleball, you're in the sagittal plane when you bend and reach forward for a dink or reach back and up for an overhead smash. You're in the frontal plane when you're at the kitchen line and you step laterally and reach quickly to your side to return the ball. You're in the transverse plane when you rotate to hit your forehand or backhand. These movement patterns can be executed at different speeds and rhythms and with varying force. You use all these patterns and qualities in pickleball.

Let's explore these three planes on our feet. This movement exploration warm-up requires your sports imagination. As kids, many of us imagined making the game-winning shot. It turns out that using our imagination to visualize in this way is a proven technique for the improvement of our sports skills. You learned all about this in the mindset chapter. For now, grab your paddle (you can also do this without your paddle), and let's look at the first plane of motion.

FORWARD AND BACKWARD (SAGITTAL PLANE)

THE DINK (FORWARD)

- Keeping your feet parallel, bend forward and imagine you are hitting a dink.
- Step forward with your right leg and dink.
- Step back with your right leg and dink.
- Repeat the sequence with the left leg.
- *Free form:* Alternate legs in any combination of patterns (you're the choreographer).
- Run forward a few steps, stop, and dink.
- Backpedal a few steps, as if you're moving out of the kitchen, stop, and dink.

BACKWARD

- Keeping your feet parallel, reach up (and slightly back for all these moves), and hit an overhead return.
- Now step forward with your right leg, reach up, and hit an overhead.
- Step back with your right leg and hit an overhead.
- Repeat the sequence with the left leg.
- *Free form:* Alternate legs in any combination of patterns (you're the choreographer).
- Run forward a few steps, stop, reach up, and hit an overhead.
- Backpedal a few steps, reach up, and hit an overhead.
- *Free form:* Alternate these movement patterns in any combination (you're the choreographer).

PICKLEBALL SPATIAL AWARENESS

As you dink, imagine the ball in front of your body. Use your paddle to make contact with the ball out in front of your body, and then close to your body. You are visualizing these challenging shots that force you to make a save from a less-than-ideal position.

As you visualize the overhead shot, make contact with the ball in front of your body, directly overhead, and behind your body.

INTEGRATE FREE FORM
- Alternate this plane's movement patterns with dinks and overheads. Now add your imagination: imagine each shot in your mind's eye.

SIDE TO SIDE (FRONTAL PLANE)

Let's explore your pickleball side to side (frontal plane) movements. A classic calisthenic for this plane is jumping jacks. Jumping jacks will be part of your dynamic warm-up.

Imagine you're standing at the kitchen line, feet parallel, and you are going to return shots.
- Reach to the side, taking the ball out of the air at shoulder level.
- Reach to waist level and return the ball.
- Reach down to knee level and return the ball. Tough one, good shot.
- Reach above the shoulder and return the ball (Ahhh, maybe it would have gone out, but you couldn't resist).
- Now get your feet moving. Shuffle a few quick steps to your paddle side and return the ball at all four levels (shoulder, waist, knee, overhead). After each return, shuffle back to your starting position.

PICKLEBALL SPATIAL AWARENESS
- In your imagination, practice hitting some shots close to your body, at a medium distance, and at full reach (your end range of motion).

INTEGRATE FREE FORM
- Now integrate all these moves in your imagination: hitting a volley, moving your feet laterally, and making returns—close, medium, and end range.

ROTATION (TRANSVERSE PLANE)

You move in rotation reach when you hit your forehand and backhand.

FOREHAND: A CROSS-STEP IN FRONT OF YOUR BODY

- Step across your body with the leg opposite your paddle hand to hit your forehand. Perform the following adjustments each time:
  - Forehand at waist level.
  - Forehand at shoulder level.
  - Forehand at knee level.

BACKHAND: A CROSS-STEP IN FRONT OF YOUR BODY

- Step across your body with the leg on the same side as your paddle hand to hit your backhand. Perform the following adjustments each time:
  - Backhand at waist level.
  - Backhand at shoulder level.
  - Backhand at knee level.

BACKSTEP FOREHAND: CROSS LEG BEHIND YOUR BODY

- From a parallel stance, step back with the leg on the same side as your paddle hand, across and behind your other leg, hit a forehand, then return to a parallel stance.

INTEGRATE FREE FORM

- Now integrate your forehands and backhands in a sequence, moving a few steps for each shot.

BACKSTEP BACKHAND: CROSS LEG BEHIND YOUR BODY

- From a parallel stance, step back with the leg opposite your paddle hand, across and behind your other leg, hit a backhand, then return to a parallel stance.

INTEGRATE FREE FORM

- Now integrate your forehands and backhands in a sequence, moving a few steps for each shot.

THE PICKLEBALL DANCE WARM-UP RECIPE

By visualizing and performing the movement patterns above, you've built the foundation of your pickleball dance. Now we're going to add some new elements, and you're going to become the Mikhail Baryshnikov or the Misty Copeland of the pickleball world. Here are added ingredients you'll use to cook up your pickleball dance warm-up.

MAKE YOUR PICKLEBALL DANCE

Here are examples of some pickleball dance routines and ways you can build your warm-up dance step by step.

THE PICKLEBALL FOOTWORK MATRIX

Imagine you are standing in the middle of a clock face. One leg at a time, step to the following numbers. This is similar to the footwork you've been doing with your PB movement patterns. After each step, return to the starting position.

Start with your right leg, then repeat with your left leg.
Do the steps three times:

Small steps.
Medium steps.
Big steps.

The Steps

Return to the starting position after each step. For each move, let the arms follow with a gesture that expresses one of the pickleball strokes.

1. Step forward to the 12.
2. Step forward and across your left leg to the 10 or 11.
3. Step right to the 3.
4. Step behind and across your left leg to the 7 or 8 (depending on your pain-free range).

THE 3-D PICKLEBALL DANCE

Create a dance with the following ingredients:

Create a sequence using the three movement patterns and all the pickleball strokes (dinks, volley, ground strokes, overheads). Include the four steps above.

Think of integrating all these elements as completing one round (similar to one round of sun salutations if you're familiar with that yoga sequence).

If you're using it as warm-up, before you play, do between 1 and 3 rounds.

Do it with a partner. Turn it into a mirror exercise where you're returning each other's imaginary shots.

FREESTYLE ROUTINES: CREATE YOUR OWN ROUTINE

The 3-D Pickleball Dance is your base. Once you've mastered this, start to add the ingredients listed below to your pickleball dance. Set the timer on your cell phone and go for 1 to 3 minutes.

More Ingredients

Weight: Add intensity to your strokes, adding power and speed (making a fist) and light drop shots (made with an open soft hand).

Levels: Bend your knees and get low for a move. Get up on your toes. Add a little jump to your routine.

Time: Change the tempo in your PB dance warm-up: Move fast and slow. Come to a complete stop. Accelerate and decelerate.

Reach: Close, medium, far—with your arms and legs.

Gaze: See the ball as it comes toward you and follow it after hitting.

PUTTING IT ALL TOGETHER: FUNDAMENTAL COURT SKILLS

How do you learn and master a new skill? Unlike the fundamental movements push and pull, sports-specific movements are complex and novel. So first we'll examine the steps for mastering sports skills. Then professional pickleball coach Wayne Dollard will instruct you on dinks, volleys, ground strokes, serves, and some basic strategies to integrate into your game.

INTEGRATION: YOUR WORKOUTS HELP YOUR GAME, YOUR GAME HELPS YOUR WORKOUTS

When an athlete makes a great play, you see the overall movement—agility, balance, speed, and grace. But you don't see all the work they put in daily—developing stability and mobility in their joints, building muscular strength and power, improving the dynamic strength of their core. Great athletes also work their drills for agility and conditioning and footwork; they complete their daily prehab, warm-ups, and cooldowns. And they stay consistent with eating healthy, cultivating a positive mindset, and ensuring they get enough sleep. Now you are the athlete, and you are developing these physical attributes and daily practices.

HOW YOU LEARN A SPORTS SKILL

We'll go into nerdish mode to talk about motor skills. (Don't stop reading. This could change you forever.) We speak of motor skills not as scientists or as PhDs in the lab but as movement practitioners. Think of this as a dinner party conversation.

Understanding the learning process can help you become your own coach. The model of skills acquisition developed by Fitts and Posner identifies three stages that we'll use to help you improve your court skills.

THE THREE STAGES

THE COGNITIVE

In this first stage, you're trying to intellectually wrap your head around what you want to learn. You are usually aware that you aren't doing the move correctly but are unsure how to make corrections. Employing language cues or images, modeling an instructor, scrutinizing videos of yourself, or watching pickleball videos on YouTube are all useful techniques at this stage. Often improvements can happen at a fast rate as you begin to understand the steps.

Strategies you can use:

- Break down the skill, maybe the serve, into smaller parts to help you understand the skill and see how the parts connect.

- Go slowly with the movement to feel it in your body, using your sensory receptor feedback loops as outlined in the sidebar "Listening to Your Body: Tuning in to Your Senses" on page 220.

- Start to connect and understand the skill's narrative—beginning, middle, and end.

- Accept frustration. Neuroscience tells us when we start to put new attention on a skill, we experience a natural period of frustration. Frustration is often the beginning of neuroplasticity. It's a good sign. You need to stay patient and take a breath. Frustration and confusion are the growing pains of learning a new skill.

THE ASSOCIATIVE

At this stage, you can grasp what is being taught and piece it together with successes and failures. You're now more in the movement lab of discovery. You're refining the game skills. You can detect the cause of errors and correct them in real time. Be aware: big leaps forward in performance are fewer at this stage as opposed to when you were a true novice. Also:

- You have a cognitive understanding of the skill.
- You are becoming freer and more fluid with your strokes.
- You can shift to external cues to help you elevate your game.
- You will always return to this stage to make improvements.
- Remember, plateaus are a good sign and let you know you are on your way to a breakthrough. Be patient; these are additional growing pains of learning a new skill.

THE AUTONOMOUS

In this stage, the skill has become almost automatic, and the performance looks effortless. Now you can home in on your performance, and your focus can shift fully to what's happening on the court. This shift is the goal—to be in the zone.

You can practice this stage by letting go and trusting your technique, playing with freedom.

BE KIND TO YOURSELF

As you're learning a new skill, it's critical to realize your focus has limits. Keep these pointers in mind:

- Keep these practice sessions relatively short: 20 to 60 minutes.
- Don't overload sessions. You can take in only so much at once: 1 to 3 goals per session.

- Write down your takeaways from the sessions.
- Take time after the session (10 minutes) to sit quietly and let the mind process what just happened. Try not to rush to the next thing immediately.

LISTENING TO YOUR BODY: TUNING IN TO YOUR SENSES

These three sensory systems will be helpful guides as you learn a new skill.

TOUCH AND FEEL (SOMATOSENSORY SYSTEM)

Gives you information about temperature, pain, and touch pressure. Touch pressure is vital; it provides information on ground force, grip pressure, and contact with the ball. Your somatosensory system is the source of comments you make, such as: "That shot felt good." "I'm getting a feel for it." "I feel grounded." Pain, obviously, is a crucial feedback message, too. If you feel what we've defined as bad pain as opposed to good pain (page 23), you should stop the session and evaluate.

SPATIAL AWARENESS (VESTIBULAR SYSTEM OR PROPRIOCEPTION)

Gives you information about where and how your body moves in space. The muscles, tendons, and joints have receptors to interpret movement and muscle force. Proprioception (often called the sixth sense) allows you to perceive the location, movement, and action of parts of the body. It plays a major role in balance, coordination, and agility. It is an awareness of position and movement through space. Great athletes are proprioception geniuses. This system answers the question: How is my body moving and organized in space?

SEEING (VISUAL SYSTEM)

Allows you to navigate the physical world and interact with the environment. Your vision allows you to read cues on the court, reacting to your opponents on the other side of the net and being in sync with your partner. This system answers the question: What is it in my environment that I should respond to?

Learning a new skill is getting a feel for it, sensing where you are in space, and connecting to environmental cues (this means seeing better on the pickleball court). These three systems gather sensory information, and we choose which ones we want to focus on. These systems can become our coaches as we go through the three stages of skill acquisition.

THE ART OF THE CUE: HOW TO COACH OURSELVES

Research shows that external cues are an invaluable tool and, for many, the most beneficial. Internal cues are also valuable when used at the right time and in the right amount. Intellectual understanding, being a student of the game, is similarly vital. Learning pickleball requires using all these tools, so we've laid out some simple principles to help.

LEVELUP CAMPS: MEET THE COACH

Now it's time to introduce your pickleball coach, Wayne Dollard. The founder of LevelUp Pickleball Camps and the publisher of *Pickleball Magazine*, Dollard is an innovator and major influencer in the pickleball world. His number one passion is designing and teaching instructional programs to help beginner and intermediate players "level up" their games. A collegiate tennis player at Penn State and a nationally ranked competitor in platform tennis, Wayne began playing pickleball four years ago. In his first year of pickleball tournaments (2018), Wayne won gold medals at the US Open, the Pittsburgh Gamma Classic, the Southpointe Classic, the Coeur d'Alene Open, and the National Championships.

Dollard explains the evolution of the LevelUp Pickleball Camps.

> **Dollard:** *When we started in 2016, we had twenty pros contributing to the curriculum. When we teach, we hear different questions. It's like a pickleball learning lab. The answers to the questions we heard over and over are now built right into our curriculum. Our teaching is now based on inputs from about seventy pros, and LevelUp camps have now taught close to 20,000 people. Our philosophy, as our name implies, is that we want people to level up at the camp. We want every person to leave significantly better than when they arrived.*

THE FUNDAMENTALS

Coach Dollard will give you an overview and tips for performing the five basic pickleball strokes, understanding basic strategies, and being a good partner.

THE CONTINENTAL GRIP

The most common grip is the continental grip. It's like a handshake grip. You grab the handle like you're shaking hands with it. It's holding the paddle the same way you would hold a hammer. For all the fundamentals in this section, you'll use the continental grip. As you play more, your grip style can change and evolve.

THE FIVE BASIC STROKES

DINKING

Your feet are wider than your shoulders; your movements are lateral; your position is a few inches behind the non-volley line (NVL).

Your hips and shoulders are square to the target.

Stay light on your feet; avoid crossing one foot over the other.

Remember that the dink shot is unique to pickleball and is NOT a "soft" decelerating full-swing ground stroke. The impact zone is inside the kitchen (not behind it).

Focus on hitting to open areas.

Keep the ball in the semicircle in front of you.

Dink with your shoulder, not your wrist, using a low to high motion (like a toss). Use soft hands with light pressure only.

Your paddle should be in front of you or parallel to your body at the start of the dink; don't take a backswing.

After drinking, get in a neutral, volley-ready position.

DINKING STRATEGIES: OFFENSE AND DEFENSE

How do you know when you are on offense or defense? You can recognize whether you are in control—on offense—by simply looking at your opponent's posture and positioning. For example, if your opponents are moving much more than you are, or the ball is outside of their semicircle, or you see them stretching, you are likely in control of the dinking exchange. The next step is to lean into the kitchen and look for an aggressive attacking opportunity.

DEFENSIVE DINKING

When you're on defense (not in control), focus on resetting the ball into a non-attackable area. Most defensive players want to use their wrists or bail out by overswinging. It's okay to back off the kitchen line to give yourself more time when receiving an aggressive dink. Just be sure to reposition back on the kitchen line and take a neutral position. And when you're on defense or pulled out of position, dinking to the middle of the kitchen is effective. Your opponents' communication skills will be tested; they may fight over the ball.

SERVING

Keep your pre-serve routine consistent and take your time.
Use your legs (big muscles) for power and lift, not just your arms.
Think "paddle head speed."
Priority is rarely placed on power but almost always on depth, getting the ball deep and
    close to the baseline .
Rotate your body so your belly button faces the target at the serve's finish. Then "pre-
    position" to open up the forehand for their third shot.
Don't be afraid to miss your serve (going long) if you have topspin.

SERVING STRATEGIES

If you can apply pressure by your serve's depth/pace/placement/variety and get free
    points by taking risks on the serve, the rewards are worth those risks.

RETURNING STRATEGIES

Start 3 to 6 feet behind the baseline.

Keep your weight on the balls of your feet; your energy comes from the legs up.

Preset your position so that the server has to serve to your favorite side.

Add plenty of net clearance to give yourself time to get up to the kitchen line.

If you are hitting hard returns and can't make it to the non-volley line in time for your fourth shot, consider hitting softer and deeper returns.

Add more clearance if you're dealing with a tough serve.

Hit your return to the player likely to be less effective with their third shot.

Or hit your return to the middle, forcing your opponents to fight over it.

LOBBING

When lobbing, don't look up; don't telegraph with a big backswing.

Use a high follow-through with the head still and down.

Lobbing is most successful when all four players are at the non-volley line.

Lob when the ball is in your body's controlled semicircular hitting area.

OVERHEADS

 ## FUNDAMENTAL FOOTWORK (LOB)

Drop the right foot back.

With arms up, point with the nondominant hand, using the index finger as a guide to spot the ball.

Turn sideways and sidestep if you have to (no crossover).

Get paddle into back scratch position.

Reach and extend for the ball; the point of contact is high.

🏓 OVERHEAD AND HIGH VOLLEY PLACEMENT

Aim: Toward the middle of the court.

Aim: At your opponent's feet unless they're behind the baseline. In that case, aim within five feet of the baseline.

If no movement is involved, you can take it out of the air in an open stance.

🏓 THIRD SHOT DROP EXPLAINED

The drop's purpose is to gain the opportunity to approach the non-volley line so that you are on even ground with your opponents.

Most intermediate players fail to understand that it is not necessary to get from the baseline to the non-volley line in just the third drop shot. Sometimes players take until the fifth and seventh to get in. A better strategy is to hit a drop, move in as much as is reasonable, then split step and be steady. People who hit one drop and run up to the non-volley line are often off-balance and miss the next shot.

DROP SHOT

The mechanics of the third shot drop are like the dink shot. Use light grip pressure only.

Use a low to high swing with the paddle head below the wrist; avoid flicking with your wrist (no wrist action).

Abbreviate the backswing and finish (paddle stays in front of the body like in a dink shot).

Think of tossing a beanbag into a cornhole (although a more side-armed motion is okay).

Carry your drops with your shoulder and legs.

The farther back you are, the more you need to step in with your opposite leg.

Trust your height and miss high, if anything; avoid any unforced errors.

THIRD SHOT STRATEGIES

Categorize when to drop or drive based on the depth of the return of serve. Be very selective in this area. So many points are lost by poor shot selection with third shot analysis. You should drive the ball:

When your opponent is only halfway to the NVL.

When your opponent is still moving.

When the return is short.

COACH DJ HOWARD:
THE INNER GAME OF PICKLEBALL

Daniel J. Howard is a nationally recognized pickleball player and top-rated coach. Daniel won gold in his first tournament in 2015, at 5.0, and since then has played many 5.0 and pro level events, winning a gold in men's 5.0 at the US Open in 2016. He is currently ranked atop the standings at 5.0 35+. His pedigree as a teacher is long. He earned a degree in exercise science and has nearly thirty years of teaching and coaching experience.

THE INNER GAME OF PICKLEBALL

Coach Howard: As a coach, I strive to get students to play intuitively rather than with their conscious mind, much like Tim Gallwey's *The Inner Game of Tennis*, but for pickleball. I want to guide them out of the conscious, logical mind and into the unconscious, intuitive, playful mind. It starts in the mind, trusting the mind to lead the body instead of overthinking. There is of course a time and a place to work on technique. This can get layered in.

The mind needs to understand the goal in simple terms. What's your target? What space are you going for on the court? If you can envision a trajectory of the ball traveling to a space, that's even better. The idea is to let your body do its thing. Knowing what target you're going for is really helpful. Otherwise, you can become too mechanical. It starts in the mind, and then the body is more apt to follow along. This type of teaching is especially helpful for the visual-based learner.

In the past, I was very much a technique guy. I studied the techniques and methods of performance for various sports. In the tennis world, I followed this model and taught the techniques of a proper swing. But my mindset has shifted in recent years, moving away from a strict focus on the mechanical techniques of a skill.

I look back at myself as a tennis pro, and I overcoached some of the techniques and didn't coach enough free play to free the mind. I needed to encourage my students to get more creative during play and figure things out independently rather than being told. In the last five years, I've learned more about the value of playing in an unconscious performance mode, letting it flow, not just focusing on physical techniques.

I also ask other questions: When you hit the shot, did you feel balanced and in a good rhythm? The desired sensation is to maintain balance, stability, and rhythm throughout the stroke. If you want to modify the stroke, add topspin or a slice, I can guide you through these strokes so you get a feeling of how they're performed. This is particularly helpful for kinesthetic learners. I can always make adjustments for different stroke pathways, angles, and speeds.

18.

CODA: INFINITE PICKLEBALL

GROW, GET BETTER

Our mantra: What's good for pickleball is good for your life.

Besides making you a better pickleball player and decreasing your chances of injury, our mission is to use pickleball as a portal to a healthy lifestyle, helping you to thrive in mind, body, and pickleball spirit for a lifetime.

On that mission, we've borrowed a concept from what the sports training world calls long-term athletic development (LTAD). LTAD is a comprehensive and systematic method for training athletes over a lifetime to optimize their potential for performance, overall well-being, and mental, emotional, and social development. Now you are that athlete.

It is never too late to start forming your athletic self. The areas of development, the basic principles, and the goals remain the same, regardless of your chronological age: have fun, move better, get stronger, practice, nourish yourself for health and performance, create a positive mindset, and integrate all the elements into the game.

ATHLETIC DEVELOPMENT: THE BIG PICTURE

Here's a summary of the big picture and takeaways from PB-150:

Play: First, you must be having fun. Playing pickleball fulfills this criterion. It is something you enjoy and have a passion for.

Movement Literacy: This stage is about moving better, developing and improving agility, balance, and coordination. As these fundamental movement skills improve, they become part of your pickleball game—they feed one another.

Strength: Getting stronger helps every aspect of life. You begin by mastering your body weight, then adding some load through dumbbells, bands, and kettlebells, or the variety of equipment available at your gym. In this stage, you also work on power and explosive strength, improving your ability to get to balls and hit winners.

Practice: In this stage, you start to integrate movement, strength, and power into pickleball drills and skills, along with incorporating your mindset techniques. Now your focus transfers from your physical skills to your game. At this level, you have made good food and nutrition choices and made them a part of your lifestyle.

The Game: It's time to have fun on the court. We've offered you some basics, but playing regular friendly matches, working with an on-court coach, and going to Pickleball camps will be helpful as you up your game.

Going Pro: This can take various forms. You may start traveling to play tournaments. You will be committed to structured practice and pregame routines, will have a regular training schedule, and will seek out competitive games locally or around the world. Fuel is key here for optimal performance.

Every Day Is Pro Day: In a fun way, you can think of every day as pro day. You follow the PB-150 program and train like a pro, integrating all the elements.

Pickleball for Life: This stage is where you make adjustments as your life and goals evolve, but you continue to integrate all the healthy aspects of wellness and sports for lifelong pickleball participation.

THINK

Thinking is another important action. Just notice all the bestselling and game-changing books devoted to it: *Atomic Habits, The Power of Habit, Mindset, Grit, The Body Keeps the Score.* And volumes more have been written on mindfulness, meditation, and cognitive behavior skills. In its own way, pickleball is an opportunity to develop a more collaborative relationship with your inner life. It provides you opportunities to check in with yourself. How do you process emotions on the court? What are your typical thought patterns (positive and negative) about a missed shot or a great one? During a game, how do you evaluate your ability to focus and manage your fears and anxieties? Any game or practice session is an opening to consider the state of your mental wellness.

PLAY

In his book *Finite and Infinite Games: A Vision of Life as Play and Possibility*, James Carse proposes two types of games: finite and infinite. "A finite game is played for the purpose of winning, and an infinite game is played for the purpose of continuing the play." Carse was a former athlete and beloved professor at New York University. In many ways, his life synthesized sports and philosophy. He passed away in 2020 just as pickleball was rising, merging sport and community during a world health crisis. This spontaneous spirit of play gave birth to the sport (created for kids on Bainbridge Island in Washington State), and its rise to combat the isolation of the pandemic represents the idea of infinite play.

Pickleball asks, What kind of player do you want to be? A finite player's main objective is to win. An infinite player's primary purpose is to continue playing. Finite players are often measured by how well they can compete, while infinite players measure their success by how well they can contribute to the collective.

The goal of an infinite game is to sustain play and to include as many participants as possible. There are no winners or losers in infinite games; the focus is on the process. Pickleball can encourage us to embrace the infinite mindset, where we recognize that life is about continuous exploration and engagement.

Infinite pickleball players (IPP) emphasize the importance of relationships. They play with others, recognizing the interconnectedness and seeking to include and uplift others. Pickleball encourages us to reflect on our own lives and the nature of play, considering finite versus infinite perspectives.

Pickleball exists on a spectrum of "it's just for fun" to extreme competitiveness. The game is unique because you'll often play doubles with a mix of talents and ages. Often, you have to choose: Do you hit killer shots at the feet of the weaker, older player, or do you play not to win but to keep the point going, challenging each other's skill level appropriately, playing truly for the joy of it, letting the finite ideas of competition fade, and hooking into something bigger, something infinite?

The same is true of your training. You can be an infinite mover. The goal of PB-150 is to get you moving better forever. Move well till you die. What better goal than that? PB-150 is just the beginning of your move-better journey toward being stronger and faster, with greater mobility, stability, and agility. Just remember, you were born to move and play.

PICKLEBALL SEXY

When my brothers and I first started playing pickleball, it was at large round-robin events. Eighty or more picklers would show up at the event, and you would play for two hours. We were exposed to players of all levels, and we were raw beginners. But we noticed true talent. We would joke, "Oh, that person was pickleball sexy."

You're pickleball sexy first and foremost by how your spirit manifests itself on the court. We were always fans of Pierre de Coubertin's vision for the Olympics. We experienced pickleball's potential to foster a similar vision. We see sports as a powerful method of promoting peaceful relations by creating a spirit of camaraderie and friendship among people from different nationalities, ages, and social and economic backgrounds. We, like Coubertin, believe that amateur athletes, who competed for the love of the sport rather than for monetary rewards, embodied the true spirit of the Games. Pickleball is a platform that can bring people together and build community.

We proclaimed someone as being pickleball sexy when they played with joy and passion, when they were focused in the moment, when they were a good sport, and when they supported their partner and respected their opponent. It's a body striving to reach its movement, strength, and grace potential. We saw a wide variety of bodies of all ages expressing themselves with athletic beauty and giving it their best effort.

We also saw people get hurt every day. This inspired us to write the book, to help pickleball players have the body to serve their pickleball spirit. This, for us, became pickleball sexy.

PART 5

The Exercise Library

Your library organizes your strength training choices in the category of your workout: Push, Pull, Squat, Lunge, Hinge, Press, Combo Lifts, Auxiliary Lifts.

19.

THE EXERCISE LIBRARY

MOVEMENT PATTERN: PUSH

Strengthens chest, shoulders, and triceps muscles and improves core stability to increase swing power.

🏓 PUSH-UPS

STARTING POSITION

Lie on your stomach; extend your legs out straight; tuck your toes. Your elbows are bent; your hands are in line with your shoulders.

Straighten your arms, lifting your entire body off the floor. Your hands and toes bear your weight.

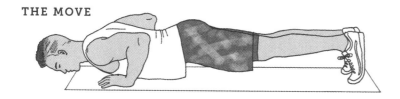

Lower your body just above the floor.

Straighten your arms to return to the starting position, completing one repetition.

VARIATION: KNEE PUSH-UPS

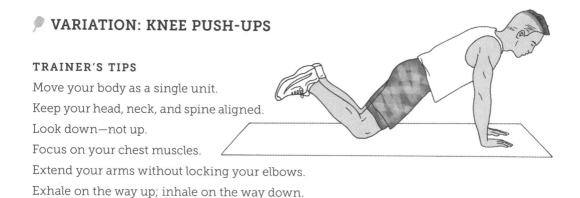

TRAINER'S TIPS

Move your body as a single unit.

Keep your head, neck, and spine aligned.

Look down—not up.

Focus on your chest muscles.

Extend your arms without locking your elbows.

Exhale on the way up; inhale on the way down.

DECLINE PUSH-UPS

STARTING POSITION

Place your feet on a bench, extending
your legs, and place your hands
on the ground directly underneath your shoulders.

THE MOVE

Lower your body until your forehead is approximately an inch from the floor.

Straighten your arms to return to the starting position, completing one repetition.

VARIATION

You may use the narrow or wide hand position.

Move your body as a single unit.

Keep your head, neck, and spine aligned.

Look down—not up.

Focus on your chest muscles.

Extend your arms without locking your elbows.

Exhale on the way up; inhale on the way down.

PUSH-UP VARIATIONS

NARROW PUSH-UPS

Lie on your stomach; extend your legs; tuck your toes. Your elbows are bent; your hands are underneath your chest about six inches apart.

Straighten your arms, lifting your entire body off the floor. Your hands and toes bear your weight.

THE MOVE

Lower your body so your chest touches the floor.

Straighten your arms to return to the starting position, completing one repetition.

VARIATION

Start on bent knees with bent elbows. Lower your body so your chest touches the floor.

Straighten your arms to return to the starting position, completing one repetition.

TRAINER'S TIPS

Move your body as a single unit.

Keep your head, neck, and spine aligned.

Look down—not up.

Focus on your chest muscles and triceps.

Extend your arms without locking your elbows.

Exhale on the way up; inhale on the way down.

🏓 WIDE PUSH-UPS

STARTING POSITION

Lie on your stomach; extend your legs; tuck your toes. Your elbows are bent; your hands
are set apart wide, anywhere from six inches to a foot outside your shoulders.
Straighten your arms, lifting your entire body off the floor. Your hands and toes bear your
weight.

THE MOVE

Lower your body so your chest touches the floor.
Straighten your arms to return to the starting position, completing one repetition.

VARIATION

Start on bent knees with bent elbows.
Lower your body so your chest touches the floor.
Straighten your arms to return to the starting position, completing one repetition.

TRAINER'S TIPS

Move your body as a single unit.
Keep your head, neck, and spine aligned.
Look down—not up.
Focus on your chest muscles.
Extend your arms without locking your elbows.
Exhale on the way up; inhale on the way down.

🏓 SINGLE-ARM WALL PUSH-UP

STARTING POSITION

Place your right hand on the wall, arm extended, leaning
into the wall at an angle.

THE MOVE

Keeping your shoulders square and core activated, lower your chest to the wall and return to the starting position.

Complete the prescribed number of reps and repeat with the other arm.

TRAINING TIPS

Keep your core activated and your body aligned and stable.

FLAT DUMBBELL CHEST PRESS

EQUIPMENT

Use a dumbbell or a kettlebell.

STARTING POSITION

Lie with your back on a bench, feet planted on the floor. Spread your feet wide to provide a stable base. With elbows bent, hold a dumbbell in each hand, positioned next to the armpits.

THE MOVE

Push the dumbbells toward the ceiling with a slight arch on a backward arc so the weight is above your eyes.

Bring the dumbbells together at the top and then lower the weights back to the armpits.

TRAINER'S TIPS

Push up to a 1 to 2 count.

Return to armpits with a controlled 3 count.

Keep your back and butt connected to the bench throughout the lift.

Exhale on the push upward; inhale on the return to starting position.

ONE-ARM DUMBBELL CHEST PRESS

EQUIPMENT

Use a kettleball or a dumbbell.

STARTING POSITION

Lie with your back on a bench, feet planted on the
    floor. Spread your feet wide to provide a stable base.

Arm bent, grasp a weight in one hand, palm facing toward your body. The weight is by
    your armpit. Place your other hand on your hip.

THE MOVE

As you push the dumbbell toward the ceiling, rotate your palm to
    face your feet. Push with a slight backward arc so the weight is
    above your eyes.

Return the dumbbell to the armpit.

Repeat with the other arm.

TRAINER'S TIPS

Push up to a 1 or 2 count.

Return to armpits with a controlled 3 count.

Keep your back and butt connected to the bench throughout the lift.

Exhale on the push upward; inhale on the return to starting position.

MOVEMENT PATTERN: PULL

Strengthens back muscles to increase your shoulder stability and swing power.

LAT PULLDOWN

EQUIPMENT
Use a lat pulldown machine or cable machine.

STARTING POSITION
Sit facing the bar and place your knees under the pads provided to
hold you down. Grab the bar, hands placed slightly wider than
shoulder width apart. Lean back slightly.

THE MOVE
Pull the bar down to chest level.
Return to the starting position, relaxing your shoulders as you do to
stretch your lats at the top.

TRAINER'S TIPS
Pull down to a 1 to 2 count.
Return to start with a stretch to a controlled 3 count.
Concentrate on using your lats and pushing your chest up toward
the bar as you pull down.
Exhale on the pull down to the chest; inhale on the return to starting
position.

PULL-UP

EQUIPMENT
A body weight exercise using a pull-up bar.

STARTING POSITION
Stand facing the bar, feet hip width apart.
Grasp the pull-up bar, hands placed shoulder width or slightly wider apart.

THE MOVE

Pull up so the bar is at chin level or
   under the chin.

Return to the starting position, relaxing shoulders to
   stretch your lats at bottom.

TRAINER'S TIPS

Pull up to a 1 to 2 count.

Return to start with a stretch to a controlled 3 count.

Concentrate on using your lats on the pull.

Exhale on the pull up to the chin; inhale on the return to
   starting position.

May be performed with a seated row machine or a cable machine.

🏓 SEATED ROW

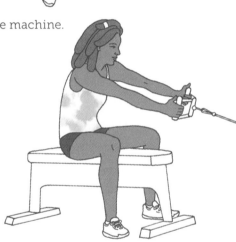

EQUIPMENT

Use a seated row machine or a cable machine.

STARTING POSITION

Sit facing the bar or handles, with feet shoulder width
   on the platform and knees bent. Lean forward and
   grab the handles.

THE MOVE

Lean back slightly in your sitting position.

Pull the bar to your chest or just below.

Push chest toward ceiling as you pull.

Return to starting position.

TRAINER'S TIPS

Pull back to a 1 to 2 count.

Return to start with a stretch to a controlled 3 count.

Concentrate on pushing your chest up as you pull the handles back toward your chest. Exhale on the pull toward the chest; inhale on the return to the starting position.

🌶 BENT DUMBBELL ROW

EQUIPMENT
Use a dumbbell or a kettlebell.

STARTING POSITION
Place your feet shoulder width apart, push your butt backward, and
    bend at the waist, keeping your shoulders above your hips. Main-
    taining a flat back, with head and spine aligned and your knees slightly
    bent, let your arm hang at your side with the dumbbell directly under your shoulder.

THE MOVE
Pull the weight up toward your hip as if you are starting a lawn
    mower.
Return the weight to hanging arm start position.
Repeat with the other arm.

TRAINER'S TIPS
Pull up on a 2 count.
Return to start to a controlled 3 count.
Keep head and spine aligned throughout.
Activate your core to keep your hip on your dumbbell side level, not letting it drop.
Exhale on the pull up; inhale on the return to starting position.

MOVEMENT PATTERN: SQUATS

Strengthen leg muscles to increase your on-court speed, power, and agility..

🏓 TRADITIONAL SQUATS

EQUIPMENT
Use dumbbells, a barbell, or your body weight only.

STARTING POSITION
If using a racked barbell, step under the barbell and grasp it, placing it
   across the meaty part of your shoulders behind your neck. If using
   dumbbells, hold them at shoulder height, palms out.
Stand with your feet shoulder width apart; point your toes slightly outward;
   unlock your knees. Distribute your weight evenly from the balls of your
   feet to your heels. Align your head, spine, and hips; your chest is out and
   your shoulders are back; your lower back is straight.
Look straight ahead; extend your arms in front of your body.

THE MOVE
Push your butt back and lower your body weight with control, as if you're sitting in a
   chair behind you.
Your thighs should be parallel to the floor; your knees and thighs form a 90-degree angle.
Stand up to return to the starting position, completing 1 repetition.

TRAINER'S TIPS
Hold dumbbells to increase the intensity.
Avoid bouncing at the bottom of the squat.
Keep your heels on the floor.
Focus on your thigh muscles.
Don't allow your hips to sway backward as you ascend.

🏓 GOBLET SQUATS

EQUIPMENT
Use a kettleball, a dumbbell, or your body weight only.

STARTING POSITION

Stand with your feet shoulder width apart; point your toes forward. Hold a
kettleball or a dumbbell in your hands between your bent arms.

Align your head, spine, and hips; your chest is out and your shoulders are
back; your lower back is straight.

THE MOVE

Push your butt back and lower your body weight with control, as if you're
sitting in a chair behind you. Your thighs should be parallel to the floor;
your knees and thighs form a 90-degree angle.

Stand up to return to the starting position, completing one repetition.

TRAINER'S TIPS

Allow the weight to travel between the knees in a vertical path.

Descend slowly, with control (count to 3).

Avoid bouncing at the bottom of the squat.

Keep your heels on the floor.

Focus on your thigh muscles.

Don't allow your hips to sway backward as you ascend.

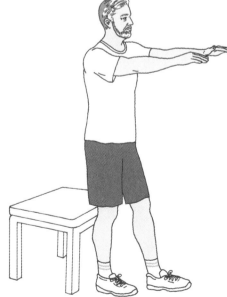

⬤ SINGLE-LEG SQUAT (MODIFIED)

EQUIPMENT

Use body weight at first; then add a dumbbell for
greater challenge.

STARTING POSITION

Stand with your back to a bench or the seat of a
chair. Your feet are hip width apart, toes forward.
Stand on one leg; straighten and raise the other
leg to a 45-degree angle.

THE MOVE

Hinging slightly at the hips, descend to the chair seat. The knee
   on the standing leg is bent; the other leg stays straight and
   off the floor. Lightly touch the chair seat with your butt.
Ascend to the starting position.
Switch legs and repeat.

TRAINER'S TIPS

Descend with control.
Don't land fully on the chair seat.
Avoid bouncing off the chair seat when you ascend.

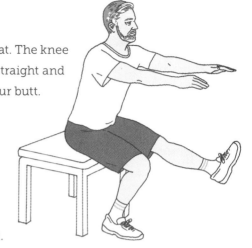

MOVEMENT PATTERNS: LUNGE

Strengthen your leg muscles to increase your speed, power, and agility.

FRONT LUNGE

EQUIPMENT

Use dumbbells, a barbell, or your body weight only.

STARTING POSITION

If using a racked barbell, step under the bar, grasp it, placing it on the meaty
   part of your shoulders behind your neck. If using dumbbells, hold them at
   shoulder height, palms out.
Stand with your feet shoulder width apart. Point your toes straight ahead;
   unlock your knees. Distribute your weight evenly from the balls of your
   feet to your heels.
Align your head, spine, and hips; your chest is out and your shoulders are
   back; your lower back is straight. Look straight ahead.

THE MOVE

Step forward with your right leg, slightly longer than your normal stride.

Lower your body weight with control, with the goal of touching your back knee to the floor. Your back leg should be under your hip; your knees and thighs form a 90-degree angle.

Push up with your front leg to return to the starting position, completing one repetition.

Options: same-leg repetitions or alternate-leg repetitions.

TRAINER'S TIP

Hold dumbbells to increase intensity.

Keep your back and neck aligned.

Descend straight down; don't sway forward.

The ultimate goal is to have the knee gently kiss the floor, but you don't have to touch the floor to gain the benefits of the exercise. Remember, always just move through a safe and pain-free range of motion.

Your knee should not extend over your toe.

Focus on your leg muscles.

Keep eyes looking straight ahead through the entire move.

⬤ BACK LUNGE

EQUIPMENT

Use dumbbells, a barbell, or your body weight only.

STARTING POSITION

If using a racked barbell, step under the bar, grasp it, placing it on your trapezius muscle (the meaty part of your shoulders behind your neck). If using dumbbells, hold them at shoulder height, palms out.

Stand with your feet shoulder width apart. Point your toes straight ahead; unlock your knees. Distribute your weight evenly from the balls of your feet to your heels.

Align your head, spine, and hips; your chest is out and your shoulders are back; your lower back is straight. Look straight ahead.

THE MOVE

Step backward with your left leg, slightly longer than your normal stride. Lower your body weight, with control with the goal of touching your back knee to the floor. Your back leg should be under your hip; your knees and thighs form a 90-degree angle.

Push up with your front and back leg to return to the starting position, completing one repetition.

Options: same-leg repetitions or alternate-leg repetitions.

TRAINER'S TIPS

Emphasize pushing up from the back leg and the butt.

Keep your back and neck aligned.

Descend straight down; don't sway forward.

The ultimate goal, as with the front lunge, is to have the knee gently kiss the floor, but you don't have to touch the floor to gain the benefits of the exercise. Remember, always just move through a safe and pain-free range of motion.

Focus on your thigh muscles.

Keep eyes looking straight ahead through the entire move.

🏓 SIDE LUNGES

EQUIPMENT

Use dumbbells, a barbell, or your body weight only.

STARTING POSITION

If using a racked barbell, step under the bar, grasp it, placing it on your trapezius muscle (the meaty part of your shoulders behind your neck). If using dumbbells, hold them at shoulder height, palms out.

Stand with your feet shoulder width apart; point

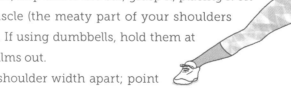

your toes forward; unlock your knees. Distribute your weight evenly from the balls of your feet to your heels.

Align your head, spine, and hips; your chest is out and your shoulders are back; your lower back is straight.

THE MOVE

Step to one side with either leg, slightly longer than your normal stride.

Land your foot heel first, then flatten your foot. Pause after stepping.

Descend until your knee and thigh form a 90-degree angle. Hold for 1 count.

Ascend, using the nonworking leg as a fulcrum, pushing back with the lead leg.

Options: same-leg repetitions or alternate-leg repetitions.

TRAINER'S TIPS

Keep your torso forward.

Keep your back and neck aligned.

Descend straight down; don't sway forward.

The knee should not extend over the toe.

Push back—not with lead leg.

MOVEMENT PATTERN: HINGE

Strengthen your glutes and back muscles and improve alignment and core stability.

🍖 ROMANIAN DEADLIFT

EQUIPMENT

Use a barbell, a kettlebell, dumbbells, or your body weight only.

STARTING POSITION

Stand with your feet hip width apart, your toes pointed forward, your knees soft. Hold the weight in front of you; your extended arms hang down.

Align your head, spine, and hips; your chest is out and your shoulders are back; your lower back is straight.

THE MOVE

Keeping the weight close to your body, hinge forward at the hips. Maintain a flat back as you hinge, keeping knees soft. Hinge until the weight reaches below your knees.

With a flat back, hinge hips forward to return to starting position.

TRAINER'S TIPS

Contract your abs to support your flat back.

Move with control, feeling the hamstrings and glutes activate.

After you ascend, your shoulders should roll back; your chest should be out.

KETTLEBELL OR DUMBBELL SWING

EQUIPMENT

Use a kettleball or a dumbbell.

STARTING POSITION

Assume a good athletic position with knees bent, feet shoulder width or a little wider apart. Hinge forward slightly from the hips, back flat, shoulders back.

Hold the kettlebell or dumbbell (vertically) in your hands, arms straight, the weight hanging between your legs.

THE MOVE

Keeping your arms straight, bring hips forward to a full extension while swinging the weight forward and up.

Return to the starting position and repeat for required reps.

Keep your arms straight throughout.

Align your head, spine, and hips; your chest is out and your shoulders are back; your lower back is straight.

Focus on pushing the kettlebell or dumbbell forward.

Exhale on the push forward; inhale on the return to starting position.

GOOD MORNINGS

EQUIPMENT

Use a barbell, dumbbells, or your body weight only.

STARTING POSITION

If using a racked barbell, step under the bar, grasp it, placing it on your trapezius muscle (the meaty part of your shoulders behind your neck). If using dumbbells, hold them at shoulder height, palms out.

Stand with feet hip width apart, toes pointed forward, knees soft.

THE MOVE

Hinge forward at the hips, back flat and knees soft.

Bend until your torso is parallel to the floor (forms a 90-degree angle with your body).

Ascend by raising your torso, back flat, back to starting position.

TRAINER'S TIPS

Contract your abs to support your flat back.

Move with control, feeling the hamstrings and glutes activate.

Squeeze your butt as you ascend.

MOVEMENT PATTERN: PRESS

Strengthen your shoulders and overhead stability.

STANDING SHOULDER PRESS

EQUIPMENT
Use a barbell, dumbbells, or your body weight only.

STARTING POSITION
Stand with your feet hip width apart, your toes pointed forward, your knees soft.

If using a racked barbell, face it and grasp it with hands that are wider than shoulder
width. If using dumbbells, hold them at shoulder height, palms out.

THE MOVE
Raise the weight directly overhead until your arms are straight.

Lower the weight with control to the starting position.

TRAINER'S TIPS
Maintain good posture throughout the
movement (avoid arching the back).

Avoid locking the elbows at the
movement.

SINGLE-ARM VARIATION
Perform one arm at a time.

MOVEMENT PATTERN: COMBO LIFTS

Increase your strength and power by training multiple muscles through whole body movement patterns.

HINGE TO UPRIGHT ROW TO PUSH PRESS

STARTING POSITION

Stand with your feet hip width apart, your toes pointed forward, your knees soft. Hold the weight in front of you; your extended arms hang down.

Align your head, spine, and hips; your chest is out and your shoulders are back; your lower back is straight.

THE MOVE

Keeping the weights close to your body, hinge forward at the hips.

Maintain a flat back as you hinge, keeping knees soft.

Hinge until weight reaches below your knees.

With a flat back, hinge hips forward to return to starting position.

Once you have returned to starting position, pull the bar, dumbbells, or kettlebells up under your chin. Rotate your elbows under the bar, dumbbells, or kettlebells. From this position, do a quarter squat and then explode back up through your toes as you push the bar, dumbbells, or kettlebells over your head.

Return to starting position and repeat the entire sequence again for the required number of reps.

TRAINER'S TIPS

Contract your abs to support your flat back.

Move with control, feeling the hamstrings and glutes activate.

Keep back straight and supported as you extend back up.

Pull the elbows toward the ceiling on the upright row.

The elbows should be beside or behind the ears at top of the push press.

Breathe in when overcoming gravity.

Breathe out when gravity is assisting.

🏓 ROTATION SNATCH

STARTING POSITION

Assume a good athletic position with knees bent, feet shoulder width apart or a little wider. The upper torso is bent forward from the hips. Your back is flat with your shoulders pulled back.

In one hand, hold a kettlebell or a dumbbell straight down in front, hanging between the legs.

THE MOVE

Push hard from the ground up so that you extend up on your toes and your hips push forward and up. At the same time, your trapezius on the side of the arm that has the weight shrugs explosively.

This first explosion is immediately followed by the arm with the weight pulling the weight toward the chin and then rotating the weight as it is pressed overhead to finish just behind or even with the ear.

Return to the start position and repeat for the required reps; then perform with the other arm.

TRAINER'S TIPS

Keep the arm straight until the first explosion with the legs and the trapezius has occurred.

Keep your head, neck, and spine aligned.

Focus on exploding the weight up toward the chin as your first explosive movement is ending.

The movement of the weight as it explodes should happen as one motion until it finishes above the head.

Exhale on the explosion up; inhale on the return to starting position.

MOVEMENT PATTERN: AUXILIARY LIFTS

Strengthen smaller muscles for improved performance and reducing risk of injuries.

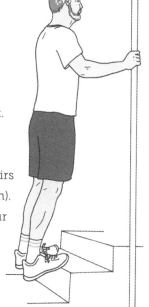

🥄 CALF RAISE

Strengthen your calves.

May be performed with a kettlebell, a dumbbell, or body weight.

STARTING POSITION

Stand with feet hip width apart, heels hanging off a bench or stairs (fully stretched), feet pointed straight ahead (neutral position). Your weight should be placed toward your big toe, with your knees slightly bent.

THE MOVE

Raise your heels up as high as possible while
distributing your weight toward your big
toe. Hold for a count. Then return to the
starting position in a 3 count.

VARIATION

May be performed one leg at a time.
May be performed with toes pointed in
(inversion) or out (eversion).

TRAINER'S TIPS

When using resistance, keep your torso
erect.
Extend through a full range of motion.
Control your speed in the downward
phase.
Always keep your weight over the balls of the feet.
Employ a full stretch in the downward motion.

🏓 LATERAL RAISE

Strengthen your shoulders.
May be performed with a kettlebell or a dumbbell.

STARTING POSITION

Stand with your feet shoulder width apart and your knees slightly
bent, your arms straight at your sides, a dumbbell in each hand.
Your hands can be neutral (thumbs facing forward), pronated (thumbs
facing in), or supinated (thumbs facing out).

THE MOVE

Raise both dumbbells to the side until they reach shoulder level. Lower slowly to starting position.

VARIATION

May be performed seated.

TRAINER'S TIPS

Maintain good posture throughout the exercise.

Avoid arching your lower back as you lift. Support your mid-section with your abdomen throughout exercise.

Keep your shoulders down and your trapezius disengaged throughout the exercise.

Focus on the sides of your shoulders.

Keep your elbows slightly bent throughout the movement.

POST DELT RAISE

Strengthen your shoulders.

May be performed with a kettlebell or a dumbbell.

STARTING POSITION

Stand with your feet shoulder width apart and your knees slightly bent, your arms straight at your sides, a dumbbell in each hand. Hold the dumbbells so that they hang at your sides, behind your lower legs, hands neutral (thumbs facing forward), and arms slightly bent. Bend forward at the waist so that your chest is a couple of inches above your knees. Your back should be flat, and your head should be in alignment with your back.

THE MOVE

Keeping your chest down and back flat, raise both dumbbells up (not back) until they are parallel to the ground, or close to parallel. Lower slowly to starting position.

Maintain your body position throughout the exercise.

Avoid arching your lower back as you lift.

Think of bringing your elbows toward your ears as you raise the dumbbells.

🌢 BENCH DIPS

Strengthen triceps.

May be performed with a weight in your lap.

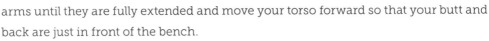

STARTING POSITION

Sit on the side of a bench. Place your palms (fingers
  forward) on the bench beside your hips. Your legs
  should be bent at the knees. Push up with both
  arms until they are fully extended and move your torso forward so that your butt and
  back are just in front of the bench.

THE MOVE

Bend your arms to a 90-degree angle, lowering your butt to the floor. Then raise yourself
  up to the starting position.

VARIATION

You can make this exercise more difficult in a variety of ways: (1) Extend your legs forward until they are straight. (2) Place a weight plate on your lap. (3) Have a partner
  press down on your shoulders as you press up.

TRAINER'S TIPS

Keep your back flat and your chest raised throughout the exercise.

Move in a strict vertical line. Do not let your hips slide forward.

Keep the forearms vertical throughout the exercise.

Don't bounce at the bottom of the movement.

Focus your mind on your triceps.

CURLS

Strengthen biceps.

May be performed with a barbell, kettlebells, or dumbbells.

STARTING POSITION

Stand with your feet shoulder width apart and your knees
slightly bent, holding a barbell, a kettlebell, or a dumbbell with an underhand grip. Hands should be about
shoulder width apart and arms fully extended down.

THE MOVE

Curl the weights in an arc toward your chin. As your
forearms reach perpendicular, elevate your elbows
slightly and contract your biceps at the top of the movement. Slowly lower the weights to the starting position.

VARIATION

If you're using a barbell, you can place your hands in a wide or a narrow grip.

TRAINER'S TIPS

Maintain good posture throughout the exercise.

Maintain a smooth movement throughout. Avoid jerky motions.

Avoid throwing the weight upward.

Keep your elbows tight to the body.

Focus your mind on your biceps.

🏓 WRIST CURLS

Strengthen your forearms and wrists.

May be performed with a barbell, kettlebells, or dumbbells.

STARTING POSITION

Sit on a bench, leaning slightly forward from the waist. Grasp the
weights, resting your forearms on the tops of your thighs, with
your palms facing up. Your hands should be hanging over your knees.

THE MOVE

Keeping your back straight and your head in line with your spine, lower the
weight by allowing hands to drop until they are fully extended. Once
the bottom of the stretch is reached, move the weight upward by
lifting your hands as high as possible while keeping your forearms
on your thighs. Repeat for prescribed reps.

VARIATION

May be performed with one arm or both arms.

TRAINER'S TIPS

Keep your forearms in contact with your thighs throughout the exercise.

Concentrate on using your wrists and forearms, not your biceps, throughout the exercise.

Keep good posture.

🏓 REVERSE WRIST CURLS

Strengthen your forearms and wrists.

May be performed with a barbell, kettlebells, or dumbbells.

STARTING POSITION

Sit on a bench, leaning slightly forward from the waist. Grasp the
weights, resting your forearms on the tops of your thighs, with your
palms facing down. Your hands should be hanging over your knees.

THE MOVE

Keeping your back straight and your head in line with your spine, lower the weight by allowing your hands to drop until they are fully extended. Once the bottom of the stretch is reached, move the weight upward by lifting your hands as high as possible while keeping your forearms on your thighs. Repeat for prescribed reps.

VARIATION

May be performed with one arm or both arms.

TRAINER'S TIPS

Keep your forearms in contact with your thighs throughout the exercise.
Keep good posture.
Focus on wrists and forearms.

For more information and videos, visit our Pickleball Hub at CompleteBookofPickleball.com.

Acknowledgments

Like Pickleball itself, the realization of this book was a team effort. It brought together an exceptional community of experts for whom we'd like to express our gratitude.

For starters, we would like to thank the entire team at Avery who gave this book a life—from Megan Newman, senior vice president and publisher, to the art department, the designers, and the copy editors. From the beginning, we felt their collaborative support for the project—the sense of security when people have your back—and the confidence their expertise inspired at each phase.

We especially thank our editor, Hannah Steigmeyer, whose steady, supportive leadership and energy were present throughout the process. She also always knew the right moments to add humor and inspire confidence.

We also want to express appreciation for our tireless and talented illustrator, Alexis Seabrook, who created and animated our cast of fitness models.

We are very grateful to all the experts who gave their time and knowledge to the book. Each one had a giving attitude, generously sharing their hard-won skills to help others. They will be an ongoing resource for the pickleball community.

We also want to thank the following: Trish Keller, an important team member, for her insights, notes, and feedback on each chapter, and for our conversations about the scope and vision of the book. Tracy Marx, for her help and feedback throughout all stages of the process. Darlene Parker, for her assistance on the BAM sketches. Elizabeth Skrobarczyk, for her feedback and thoughts on nutrition. Drusilla Brungardt, for her willingness to test the routines.

As always, many thanks to our mother, Joyce, and our aunt June, who supplied food, cooking, coffee, conversation, and entertainment during an important writing phase that took place in our Kansas hometown. They allowed, for a period of time, the house we all grew up in to become a pickleball writing factory.

Finally, thanks to the entire team at Trident Media, with a shout-out to Claire Romine for insights and support. And, of course, our agent, Dan Strone (cofounder of Trident), for his vision, enthusiasm, and invaluable guidance on the book.

Resource List

OUR TEAM OF EXPERTS

Peggy Brill
  brillpt.com

Dr. Patrick Cohn
  https://www.peaksports.com/sports-psychology-for-pickleball/

Josh Dines
  https://www.hss.edu/
  https://www.hss.edu/physicians_dines-joshua.asp

Wayne Dollard
  www.leveluppickleballcamps.com
  and
  www.pickleballmagazine.com

Byron Holmes
  yourspineonpickleball@gmail.com

Daniel J. Howard
  danieljpickleball.com

Dr. Daniel Laby

https://sportsvision.nyc/

Dr. Arash Maghsoodi

https://theprehabguys.com/

Will Sevening

wsevening@Spurs.com

Jaclyn Sklaver

www.athleatsnutrition.com

Dr. Keith Smithson

Sportsvisionpros.com

Notes

CHAPTER 1: YOUR PICKLEBALL ATHLETIC JOURNEY

9 **This duration is based on what exercise scientists:** U.S. Department of Health and Human Services, *Physical Activity Guidelines for Americans*, 2nd ed. (Washington, DC: U.S. Department of Health and Human Services, 2018), 8, https://health.gov/sites/default/files/2019-09/Physical_Activity_Guidelines_2nd_edition.pdf.

12 **Michelangelo's Moses:** Dr. Beth Harris and Dr. Steven Zucker, "Michelangelo, *Moses*," Smarthistory: Center for Public Art History, https://smarthistory.org/michelangelo-moses/.

CHAPTER 2: TRAINING PRIMER

14 **according to a 2018 survey:** Daniel E. Lieberman, "How to Make Exercise Happen," *Harvard Gazette*, February 5, 2021, https://news.harvard.edu/gazette/story/2021/02/in-new-book-daniel-lieberman-examines-what-motivates-us-to-exercise/.

14 **Lieberman defines exercise:** Daniel E. Lieberman, *Exercised: Why Something We Never Evolved to Do Is Healthy and Rewarding* (New York: Pantheon, 2020).

16 **The general adaptation syndrome (GAS):** M. Jackson, "Evaluating the Role of Hans Selye in the Modern History of Stress," in *Stress, Shock, and Adaptation in the Twentieth Century*, eds. David Cantor and Edmund Ramsden (Rochester, NY: University of Rochester Press, 2014), https://www.ncbi.nlm.nih.gov/books/NBK349158/.

23 **"The exercise is the assessment":** Dr. David Tiberio, "The Evolution of Functional Testing," Gray Institute, September 1, 2016, https://www.grayinstitute.com/blog/the-evolution-of-functional-testing.

CHAPTER 5: PB-150 WORKOUT PLANNER

54 **goal-setting model was first developed:** Peter Drucker, *The Practice of Management* (New York: HarperBusiness, 1954). While Drucker proposed objective-setting as a management practice, others have been credited with developing the SMART acronym, including George T. Doran.

58 **Researchers found that participants who focused:** Joaquin Calatayud et al., "Importance of Mind-Muscle Connection during Progressive Resistance Training," *European Journal of Applied Physiology* 116, no. 3 (2016): 527–33, doi: 10.1007/s00421-015-3305-7.

CHAPTER 6: PREHAB

61 **Medical injury costs for pickleball:** Alexa Mikhail, "Pickleball Has Been a Lifeline for Seniors, but the Sport's Injuries May Cost Americans Nearly $400 Million This Year," *Fortune Well*, June 27, 2023, https://fortune.com/well/2023/06/27/pickleball-injuries-may-cost-americans-nearly-400-million -this-year/.

CHAPTER 7: DYNAMIC WARM-UP

69 **decrease your risk of injury by up to 30 percent:** David Sadigursky et al., "The FIFA 11+ Injury Prevention Program for Soccer Players: A Systematic Review," *BMC Sports Science, Medicine and Rehabilitation* 9 (2017): article number 18, doi: 10.1186/s13102-017-0083-z.

69 **questioning the benefits of static stretching:** David G. Behm et al., "Acute Effects of Muscle Stretching on Physical Performance, Range of Motion, and Injury Incidence in Healthy Active Individuals: A Systematic Review," *Applied Physiology, Nutrition, and Metabolism* 41, no. 1 (2016): 1–11, doi: 10.1139 /apnm-2015-0235.

70 **The static vs. dynamic stretch debate:** https://www.ideafit.com/personal-training/pre-exercise -stretching-and-performance/.

70 **causes synovial fluids to flow:** David Sadigursky et al., "The FIFA 11+ Injury Prevention Program for Soccer Players: A Systematic Review."

70 **dynamic movement is effective:** Victor Moreno-Pérez et al., "Post-Activation Performance Enhancement of Dynamic Stretching and Heavy Load Warm-up Strategies in Elite Tennis Players," *Journal of Back and Musculoskeletal Rehabilitation* 34, no. 3 (2021): 413–23, doi:10.3233/BMR-191710.

70 **a fluid mind-body conversation:** David G. Behm, *The Science and Physiology of Flexibility and Stretching: Implications and Applications in Sport Performance and Health* (London: Routledge, 2018), https://doi.org/10.4324/9781315110745.

CHAPTER 11: COOLDOWN

84 **RPE developed by Dr. Gunnar Borg:** "What Is RPE?" Jump Start by WebMD, Dan Brennan, reviewer, November 27, 2021, https://www.webmd.com/fitness-exercise/what-is-rpe.

133 **In a 2016 study, Dr. Helene Langevin:** L. Berrueta, et al., "Stretching Impacts Inflammation Resolution in Connective Tissue," *Journal of Cellular Physiology* 231, no. 7 (2016): 1621–27, doi.: 10.1002/jcp.25263.

133 **The Italian team wired participants:** Luciano Bernardi et al., "Effect of Rosary Prayer and Yoga Mantras on Autonomic Cardiovascular Rhythms: A Comparative Study," *British Medical Journal* 323, no. 7327 (2001): 1446–49, doi: 10.1136/bmj.323.7327.1446.

133 **Two American researchers, Dr. Richard Brown and Dr. Patricia Gerbarg:** Richard P. Brown and Patricia L. Gerbarg, *The Healing Power of the Breath: Simple Techniques to Reduce Stress and Anxiety, Enhance Concentration, and Balance Your Emotions* (Boston: Shambhala, 2012).

CHAPTER 12: FOAM ROLLING

140 **"Fascia is the Cinderella of body tissues":** Sarah Berry, "Cinderella Tissue: The Most Critically Ignored Part of the Body?" *Sydney Morning Herald*, August 12, 2014, https://www.smh.com.au/lifestyle/health -and-wellness/cinderella-tissue-the-most-critically-ignored-part-of-the-body-20140806-100xw3 .html.

142 **The good news is foam rolling:** Graham Z. MacDonald et al., "An Acute Bout of Self-Myofascial Release Increases Range of Motion without a Subsequent Decrease in Muscle Activation or Force," *Journal of Strength and Conditioning Research* 27, no. 3 (2013): 812–21, doi: 10.1519/JSC.0b013e31825c2bc1.

CHAPTER 13: INTRODUCING PICKLEBALL WELLNESS

151 **Dunn took the word *well-being*:** Halbert L. Dunn, "High-Level Wellness for Man and Society," *American Journal of Public Health* 49, no. 6 (1959), https://www.ncbi.nlm.nih.gov/pmc/articles/PMC1372807/pdf/amjphnation00322-0058.pdf.

153 ***Forbes* and *The Desert Sun* both report:** Mary Barsaleau, "Move Over Golf, Pickleball Is the New Way to Network," *Desert Sun*, November 12, 2022, https://www.desertsun.com/story/sports/2022/11/12/pickleball-new-way-network/10675266002/.

154 **The act of playing:** Stuart Brown and Christopher Vaughan, *Play: How It Shapes the Brain, Opens the Imagination, and Invigorates the Soul* (New York: Avery, 2009).

CHAPTER 15: THE PICKLEBALL MINDSET

184 **"We found in our laboratory":** Andrew Huberman, "Breathing Techniques to Reduce Stress and Anxiety: Dr. Andrew Huberman on the Physiological Sigh," *The Tim Ferriss Show*, YouTube video, 4:47, July 8, 2021, https://www.youtube.com/watch?v=kSZKIupBUuc.

186 **"The core of mental toughness":** Nathaniel Erickson, "Brené Brown Says This Is the 'Core of Mental Toughness,'" *USA Today*, November 11, 2022, https://ustoday.news/brene-brown-says-this-is-the-core-of-mental-toughness/.

CHAPTER 16: YOUR PICKLEBALL SPORTS MEDICINE TEAM

191 **Even health insurance companies:** Alexa Mikhail, "Pickleball Has Been a Lifeline for Seniors, but the Sport's Injuries May Cost Americans Nearly $400 Million This Year," *Fortune Well*, June 27, 2023, https://fortune.com/well/2023/06/27/pickleball-injuries-may-cost-americans-nearly-400-million-this-year/.

CHAPTER 17: PUTTING IT ALL TOGETHER: FUNDAMENTAL COURT SKILLS

218 **developed by Fitts and Posner:** Will Shaw, "Fitts & Posner's Stages of Learning—Cognitive, Associative and Autonomous," *Sports Science Insider*, January 20, 2021, https://sportsscienceinsider.com/stages-of-learning/.

CHAPTER 18: CODA: INFINITE PICKLEBALL

231 **A finite game is played:** James P. Carse, *Finite and Infinite Games: A Vision of Life as Play and Possibility* (New York: Free Press, 1986).

Index

Page numbers in *italics* refer to figures and tables.

balance
- and core training, 101
- and dynamic warm-ups, 70
- and overview of PB-150 program, 45–46, 49
- and PB-150 drills, 116, 117–18, 120, 122–29
- and pickleball wellness, 151, 211
- self-assessment, 24
- and strength training, 83

balanced meals, 167

BAM (Basic Athletic Measurement) protocols, 198

barbells, 246, 248–51, 253–54, 261–62

baseline
- and drop shots, 225
- and mental rehearsal, 182
- and overhead shots, 225
- and PB-150 drills, 126–28
- and pickleball combine testing, 29, 33–35, 37
- and return shots, 224
- and serves, 223

Basic Athletic Measurement (BAM Testing), 4, 26

bench dips, 260

benchmarking, 26

benefits of pickleball, 5

bent dumbbell row, 245

berries, 166, 172

biceps, 65, 132, 185, 261, 262

bicycle exercise, 104, 107

bicycle exercise, 104, 107

big toe down exercise, 197

big toe up exercise, 197

bioavailability of supplements, 161–62

biomechanics, 119

bird dog exercise, 104, 110–11

Black Bean Chili-Stuffed Sweet Potatoes with Ground Turkey, 174–75

blood flow, 198

body awareness
- and foam rolling, 141, 144
- and inner game of pickleball, 227
- and PB-150 drills, 116–17
- and prehab routine, 62
- and rating of perceived exertion, 85–86

and self-training goal, 13

and sports skill learning process, 218, 220

body composition, 151

body temperature, 70

body weight, 117

body zones, 202–3

bone strength, 83

Borg, Gunnar, 84

BPA-free bottles, 161

Brady, Tom, 8

brain health, 154

breakfast foods, 171

breathing
- breathing techniques, 18
- and cooldown routine, 133–34
- and foam rolling, 143
- and progressive muscle relaxation, 185

Breath: The New Science of a Lost Art (Nestor), 134

Brill, Peggy, 4, 192

Brill Chicken exercises, 205–6

bronchitis, 165

Brown, Brené, 186

Brown, Richard, 133–34

Brown, Stuart, 153

Brungardt, Brett, 4

Brungardt, Mike, 4

butt kick exercise, 79

C

calisthenics, 213

calves
- calf exercises, 87–100, 257–58
- calf stretch exercise, 64
- and foam rolling, 143, 144

cancer, 133

canned goods, 171

carbohydrates
- anti-inflammatory turmeric protein shake, 169
- and hydration drinks, 160
- key sources of, 156–57
- and meal schedules, 167

cardiovascular system, 194–95

carioca exercise, 79–80, 204

carotenoids, 165

Carse, James, 231

casein, 162

cat cow stretch, 136

center of gravity

and dynamic warm-ups, 71

and PB-150 drills, 116–18, 120

See also balance

cereals, 171

cervical spine, 207

Chia Seed Protein Pudding, 172–73

Chicken N Pickle, 153

child's pose, 137

chili recipe, 174–75

choline, 165

chronic disease, 83

chronic obstructive pulmonary disease (COPD), 165

circulation, 70, 198

Clean 15 guidelines, 159

cobra stretch, 136

cognitive function, 83, 186–87, 211, 218–19, 231

Cohn, Patrick, 4, 179–80, 181–83, 187, 190

collagen, 163–64

combine testing
- analyzing numbers, 38–40
- four-way agility, 28–30
- leveling up, 40–42
- metrics for, 26–27
- and pickleball fitness, 8
- pickleball sprint, 36–38
- power core, 34–36
- reaction shuttle, 30–32, *31*
- standing broad jump, *33*, 33–34
- tests, 28–40

combining workouts, 50

combo lifts, 255–57

compensation, 209

competition range of motion, 132

complex carbohydrates, 156

condiments, 171

conditioning
- and court skills, 217
- and frequency of training, 17
- and movement literacy, 115–19
- and overview of PB-150 program, 46–47, 51–52
- and PB-150 drills, 120–21, 122–29
- and PB-150 workout planner, 53

confidence, 180–81

connective tissues
- and cooldown routine, 133
- and dietary collagen, 163–64

exercise physiology, 20
exhaustion, 16, 26
expectations, 186–87
explosive system, 20
extension motion, 208, 210
external cues, 221

F

fascia, 119, 140–42
fast feet exercise, 80
fast training speeds, 19
fats, dietary, 157, 167
fatty fishes, 166
fear of failure, 187–88
feet, 144, 197–98
fiber, dietary, 156, 174
fig bars, 170
figure-4 squat, 76
Finite and Infinite Games
   (Carse), 231
fish oils, 162
fitness, 8, 14–15, 196–97
flat dumbbell chest press, 241
flexibility
   and cooldown routine, 10, 133
   full range of motion, 18
   and overview of PB-150
      program, 46
   and pickleball wellness, 154
flexion motion, 208, 210
flow state, 153
foam rolling, 10, 46–47, 49, 139–47
focus, mental, 182–83
focus, visual, 201
footwork
   and court skills, 217
   and dance exercises, 215
   and footwork lob, 224
   and PB-150 drills, 123–29
Forbes, 153
forearms, 262
forehand stroke, 120, 208,
   210–11, 213–14, 223
four-square hops, 127–29
four-way agility, 28–30, *29*
four-way core, 101–2
free play, 227
freestyle routines, 216
Freezer Breakfast Burritos, 176–78
frequency of training, 17–18
fried foods, 166
front lunge, 248

fruits, 166, 168, 170, 173
frustration, 218–19
functional flexibility, 210

G

Gallwey, Tim, 226
Garden of Life, 161
gaze, 216. *See also* vision
general adaptation syndrome
   (GAS), 16
Gerberg, Patricia, 133–34
glucose, 156
glutes, 103, 146, 251–53
glycolytic system, 20
goals of book, 5–6
goblet squats, 246–47
good mornings (drill), 253
grains, 166, 170
Gray, Gary, 23
Gretzky, Wayne, 200
grips, 222
ground force, 117, 118, 120
ground strokes
   and core training, 102, 113
   and dance exercises, 216
   dinks contrasted with, 222
   and PB-150 drills, 120
   and pickleball energy
      systems, 20
   and prehab routine, 81
   and self-training goal, 13
   and sports nutrition, 155
   and synergistic body
      motions, 194
guarding response to pain, 210
gut health, 163

H

habits
   and diet, 158
   and foam rolling, 139
   and mindfulness, 231
   and PB-150 workout planner, 56
   and the pickleball mindset, 179
   and pickleball wellness, 151
   and posture, 208
   and prehab routine, 69
   and recovering from
      mistakes, 189
half-circle drill, 127
half-kneeling soleus (calf)
   stretch exercise, 64

hamstrings, 135, 145
hand-eye coordination, 203
handshake grip, 222
happy pickleball spine, 210
Harris, Beth, 11
Harvard University, 133
head lift exercise, 66
healing process, 178, 194
health insurance, 191
health statistics, 14
heart health, 133, 165, 184
heel walk, 73
high-intensity interval training
   (HIIT), 5, 20
High-Level Wellness (Dunn), 151
high volley strokes, 225
hinge movements and exercises,
   87–100, 251–53, 255–56
hips
   and combo lift exercises,
      255–56
   and cooldown routine, 136–37
   and core training, 101–3,
      105–12
   and dink shots, 222
   and dynamic warm-ups,
      70–80
   and foam rolling, 139–40,
      145–46
   and hinge exercises, 251–53
   and lunge exercises, 248–51
   and pain-free pickleball
      exercises, 206
   and PB-150 drills, 116, 124,
      125, 127
   and pickleball combine
      testing, 28, 35–36, 38
   and piriformis stretch, 205
   and prehab routine, 46, 62,
      64–67
   and press exercises, 254
   and PT exercises for
      pickleball, 206–7
   and range-of-motion self-
      assessment, 23–24
   and spine exercises, 206, 207
   and squat exercises, 245–48
   and synergistic body
      motions, 194
Holmes, Bryon, 208
Hospital for Special Surgery
   (HSS), 192, 193